THE ENCHANTED ORCHARD

THE
ENCHANTED ORCHARD

AND OTHER FOLKTALES
OF CENTRAL AMERICA

Selected and adapted by

DOROTHY SHARP CARTER

Illustrated by W. T. MARS

HARCOURT BRACE JOVANOVICH, INC.
NEW YORK

ISBN 0-15-225955-4

Library of Congress Catalog Card Number: 78-187856

Printed in the United States of America

First edition

B C D E F G H I J

FOR ALBERT

CONTENTS

6   *Contents*

THE ENCHANTED ORCHARD

INTRODUCTION

In this country too little is known of Latin American literature, especially that written for children. Too few of Central and South America's children's stories are translated into English. It is our loss that they are not. In particular, the folktales of Latin America are delightful and give an insight into a different way of life, a different past, a different manner of thinking.

Some time ago I lived for four years in Central America. To me it is one of the most charming regions of the world and its people some of the friendliest. In this collection I have tried to show various aspects of Central America's heritage. The stories fall roughly into three categories: tales of Indians before the Spanish Conquest; tales of animals, which seem always to constitute a great part of folk literature; and miscellaneous tales, including fantasy and legend and custom and history of times since the Conquest.

The Indian tales are either myths, stories telling the how and why of an institution or natural phenomenon, or legends, stories coming down from the past, often regarded as true happenings. Five stories are taken from the *Popol Vuh*, ancient book of the Quiché Maya Indians, whose dominion extended through what is now Guatemala.

The animal tales concern animals found in Central America, the most popular figure being Tío Rabbit. "Tío" means Uncle and "Tía" Aunt, but sometimes animals are called " 'Mano" and " 'Mana," meaning Brer and Sis. Often, similar animal stories are claimed by various countries; for instance, Brer Rabbit, of Uncle Remus fame, is found through Latin America with slight variations.

The post-Conquest tales show the impact of Christianity and the influence of the European fairy tale.

Some of the words in the tales either cannot be translated or are used so often—such as *cacique*, meaning "chief"—that I have simply retained the Spanish, or local, word. This is frequently the case in the names of Central American plants, animals, and foods, such as the trees *espabel, ojoche, pubché; teosinte*, a type of grass; *palmito*, the delicious fruit of a member of the palm family; *quetzal*, a tropical bird of brilliant colors; *frijoles*, beans, and others. I have also employed the word *tigre*, or "tiger," which is used in Latin America to denote "jaguar"; similarly, the word "lion" refers to the puma.

I hope that North American children will enjoy hearing about the first wooden men and the Cegua and the Sisimiqui as much as Central American children do. And, hopefully, these stories will help in a small way to promote further interest in Latin American literature.

I would like to add here a note of thanks to Dr. Alice Brooks McGuire of the University of Texas at Austin for her guidance and encouragement, without which these folktales might never have appeared.

THE
ENCHANTED ORCHARD

Long, long ago, before Indians wore Christian names and while magic still drifted about the land, there lived a youth named Tapica—a handsome lad, industrious. Not too serious . . . but not too frivolous, either. "Stable," said the village mothers approvingly. "Not *that* stable," the village girls said, giggling.

A lucky boy, Tapica. He had the pick of the village maidens. The one he picked was so graceful that she could dance her way home, her water jug perched on her head, without spilling a drop. She could grind a measure of corn in the time of taking ten steps. She wove her own clothing and molded shapely jugs and bowls and plates of red clay. A wise boy, Tapica.

Oh yes, wise, yes indeed . . . but . . . I forgot to say. One defect she had. And that was? She wished for what wasn't. If you gave her a handful of red daisies, she wished for white. If there were beans for dinner, she asked for chilies. When a suitor brought her from the highlands of Guatemala a choice piece of jade, she thanked him nicely, but to her friends she said with a sigh, "Ah, if it had only been a different shape!" And on and on.

Fortunately, Tapica did not notice this fault. Or if he did, he thought it one common to all girls. He was merely annoyed that she put him off. And when he tried to break her water jug, as a declaration of their marriage, she ran away laughing.

One day, exasperated, he said to her, "This year I have sown two fields of corn and one of squash. I have built a cottage on the skirt of the mountain. I have labored to perfect a grinding stone pleasing to the hand. There lacks only a someone to light the hearthfire."

His sweetheart relented. "I will come to light it, Tapica," she said. "But first do one thing for me. I wish to taste of the fruit of the Orchard of Opoa Lagoon and plant the seeds in our patio. Will you get me some? Then at full moon I shall go with you to the new cottage."

The Orchard of Opoa Lagoon! Truly, the girl did not ask for little. At one time or another every villager had happened on the orchard. His mouth had watered at the orange or rosy or golden fruit hanging from the trees. But as he reached out a hand to pluck a piece, there was a little whirling noise and poof! the orchard had disappeared . . .

However, Tapica resolved to try. Lacing on his sandals of tapir hide, he hung his bow over his shoulder, stuck his obsidian knife in his sash, and set off. He, like the rest of the villagers, had from time to time been tempted by the enchanted orchard. Now he sought it where he had seen it last. Thick forest there was much of. Of the enchanted orchard, nothing.

Suddenly, after days of searching, he glimpsed the orchard, just in front of him. As he attempted to step into it, it slid away. There it was, still in sight, but distant. Again he ran toward it. Again it dissolved, so that where he should have walked on thick grass, there were only brush and vines.

Cursed orchard, thought Tapica, though he was careful not to say so aloud. The orchard spirits might well be sensitive as well as mischievous. Mischievous they were . . . he had just stumbled through a bramble patch. For himself he would have given up the mocking chase long ago. However, for his beloved . . .

The hunt continued, day after day, until one evening the orchard appeared before him, more brilliant and splendid than ever. The weary Tapica plodded toward it, certain that it would vanish. But no, he stepped onto thick grass. He reached for a ripe mango. Shiny and plump it felt in his hand. He cut it and tasted of the delicious pulp and juice. Of the many varieties of fruit, he tried one after another.

Finally, satisfied, he filled his bag with different species and hoisted it to his shoulder. Off to the village with all haste . . .

To his horror he found he could not move his feet. Dropping the bag of fruit on the ground, he pulled . . . and with no effort his feet set themselves in motion. Well!

Again he threw the bag over his shoulder. Again his feet remained nailed to the ground. Would these orchard spirits stop at nothing?

Smothering his anger, Tapica began sweetly, "Honored spirits, I, too, appreciate a good joke. Ha, ha! But since it is late and darkness already . . ."

In the murmur of a breeze winding among the trees he thought he heard the words, "Eat what you will, Tapica. But forbidden it is to carry away a single fruit. Leave the bag and depart. It is your last chance."

Tapica was furious. "And disappoint my bride? By no means. After all my running and chasing I am entitled to a few pieces. . . ." Stubbornly he held to the bag.

All at once his feet felt heavy as though knotted to the earth with long roots. Looking down, he saw his body covered with ridged bark. And even when he dropped the bag of fruit, it fell, not from fingers, but from rough twigs attached to gnarled branches. Tapica had become a part of the enchanted orchard.

THE
WARRIOR WHO SHOT
ARROWS AT A STAR

Years ago, in the time when the Mayas worshipped their god Kukulkan, whose symbol was the plumed serpent, there was a village called Yamalá.

In 1537, after centuries of existence, this Yamalá ceased to be. Why? Because it refused to pay tribute of gold to Spain. For that, Spanish soldiers came and destroyed it.

Today there remain only hills and mounds of grassy earth covering the stones that once were walls. One thing more survives—a legend carved into the rocky banks of the river Jicatuyo. The bas-relief shows a kneeling Indian warrior, his bow flexed, in the act of shooting an arrow toward the stars.

Who was this warrior, so bold or so mad as to shoot at the heavens? What story does he tell? The descendents of Yamalá know. They have heard the tale from their fathers and grandfathers and great-grandfathers.

Long before the time of the Spanish Conquest,

Yamalá flourished in its green wooded valley. Through a gorge that wound around the city flowed the Jica-tuyo River. The city was ruled by a wise and respected *cacique* of the Mayas.

This *cacique* had a daughter, Ix-Tab, of seventeen years, who was famous throughout the region for her beauty. Her hair was the bluish-black of a butterfly's wing. Her dark eyes were deep and mysterious, like the quiet pools of a river beneath the whispering oaks. Her small red mouth showed teeth shiny as mother-of-pearl.

Being of an age to marry, Ix-Tab did not lack for suitors. Youths came from far and near to make themselves agreeable, to court Ix-Tab, to prove to the *cacique* what a fine son-in-law each could be.

But Ix-Tab's father had long since arranged her marriage with a chieftain of the neighboring district of Tencoa. This was done to strengthen an alliance between the two, that they might better resist the raids of the Aztecs. Those war-hungry people streamed over the hills each year. After the crops were harvested, they sought grain and prisoners to sacrifice on the altars of their gods.

Despite such a sensible arrangement, Ix-Tab was not happy. She had been bitten by the blue fly that infects the victim with love. Unfortunately, Ix-Tab's love did not direct itself toward the Tencoan chieftain. Unreasonable as love often is, it fell meltingly about the person of Hol-Kan.

Hol-Kan was a brave and spirited warrior belonging to her own village. And he in turn loved Ix-Tab fervently.

As the girl danced in the harvest celebrations, while the balls of copal burned in the braziers and the fragrant smoke drifted about the dancers, Hol-Kan had eyes only for her. During a turn of the dance Ix-Tab found herself face to face with Hol-Kan. He turned on her a burning glance.

Ix-Tab whirled away, her heart heavy. She loved Hol-Kan. But the marriage with the Tencoan chief must be respected. A Mayan woman never rebelled against her parents, against the customs of her country, against the gods. Only an unforeseen event could change her destiny.

A few days later alarming news reached Yamalá. Aztec warriors wearing the feathers of their eagle-god were on the way to attack the Mayan serpent. As always, they sacked the Mayan towns and carried away victims to offer to their gods.

Hol-Kan, leader of the Mayan troops, ordered his men to make ready. He sent the women and children to a hidden valley where they would be safe.

Before leaving, Ix-Tab, her face wet with tears, approached Hol-Kan to bid him farewell. "May the spirit of Kukulkan be with you," she told him. "May you conquer the Aztecs and return well and unharmed. If you do not come back, I shall die of grief. My soul will fly to the heavens and there be changed into a star that will shine through the dark searching for you." Then she turned and ran back to her companions.

The Mayan force bravely engaged the enemy. But

20

the savage horde of Aztecs far outnumbered the Mayas. With their ferocious attack they scattered the
Mayan soldiers and looted the town. Cunning as they
were, they tracked the women and children to their
hiding place and there slaughtered them or took them
captive. Only a few agile ones climbed to caves in the
rocky banks and escaped the fleet arrows and obsidian
edges of the warclubs. With many others, Ix-Tab per-
ished under the brutal attack.

When at last Hol-Kan managed to gather his
troops together and return to battle, it was too late.
They found only the smoking ashes of their homes and
the little valley filled with dead.

Mad with grief, Hol-Kan raised his face to the
skies. His eye caught a small blue star that twinkled in
the firmament as if blinking at him. The disordered
mind of the warrior believed that the little star was Ix-
Tab's spirit, beckoning to him.

From that time on, Hol-Kan would climb each
evening to the top of a mountain. Aways he carried
with him a quiverful of arrows. With his bow aimed at
the sky, he would send arrow after arrow flying toward
the blue star, hoping to dislodge it.

At times vapors drifted across the heavens. Lightning illuminated the sky. Shooting stars set the darkness on fire before vanishing over the horizon. The
poor warrior would shake and cry out with excitement,
believing that his arrows were coming closer to the
blue star. And the villagers would murmur, "It is Hol-
Kan, turning loose the stars from their pasture."

One night Hol-Kan, shooting with great force,

loosed an arrow at the very instant that a shooting star fell toward earth. Hol-Kan happened to glimpse its image reflected in a quiet pool of the river. His blue star had finally been freed and had fallen into the water!

Hol-Kan threw himself from the high bank into the river. But the waters were too shallow. The Indian was killed on the jumbled rocks. The people of Yamalá buried him beside Ix-Tab and carved his likeness on the riverbank.

In spite of the centuries that have passed, one can still see the figure of Hol-Kan engraved on the rock. And the people tell of Yamalá and Ix-Tab and the warrior who shot arrows at a star.

THE
BOY WITH THE HAND
OF FIRE

During the nights of winter, when Zi-ije, the moon, disappears from the sky and the lightning takes her place, it is time to think of the boy—the boy who kneels there above, streaking the clouds with his hand of fire. And how did he get there, that boy?

The white-haired storyteller nods to himself. Listen, listen, and I will tell you. It happened in the time of our enemies the Muerras, who lived in the Sand Mountain.

One day many of our grandfathers entered the forest to hunt the tapir that bathed in the distant streams.

They heard suddenly a loud, terrible noise—a noise as if a herd of tapirs were hurtling through the thick brush. The warriors raised their lances. They raised their war clubs. They rushed forward to kill the animals so that they might return home with meat. But instead of tapirs, they were horrified to see crawling toward them out of the mountain a great serpent.

The chief overcame his fear. Quick as a hawk from heaven, he killed the enormous snake. At once he called to his warriors who had fled, "Come, come, I have killed the serpent! Come and see for yourselves."

The warriors, rejoicing to hear their leader's voice, gathered around to see the snake. They saw and trembled. They saw and were astonished. As all were hungry, the chief invited them to eat of the serpent's flesh. Despite their fright, they all ate except for a boy—a boy who had come with them on his first hunt.

Having finished, they lay down to rest and sleep. When the new day arose from the sea, the boy who had not eaten of the Zaálan, or serpent, found that all his companions had been turned into snakes. Without doubt it was the work of their enemies the Muerras, who dwelt in the Sand Mountain. What a calamity! What a disaster!

The boy shivered when he heard the snakes speak to him. "Have no fear. Be not afraid. Listen to us without departing. We go now to the hill of Tojivachaca. Return to your town and tell them what has happened to us. Tell them, too, what must be done later, what they must do to disenchant us when we come next summer during the drought."

The boy carried in his head the words of his bewitched companions; he ran to deliver them to the people of his town. He spoke of what had taken place to the chief and his warriors.

When the next summer arrived, in the time of drought, many Zaálan appeared in the town. The Indians wept on seeing their relatives mutely dragging themselves over the hot dust.

The Enchanted Orchard

In the midst of their weeping the boy cried, "They desire you to strike off their heads. They desire you to stretch their bodies beneath the leaves. In that way, in the time of storms, they will change back to themselves. This is what it is necessary to do. This must you do to free them from the spell of our enemies the Muerras."

The boy spoke these words and then again and yet again. But . . . who could bring himself to cut off the head of his relative, even if enchanted?

The snakes became enraged because no one would obey their words. One, perhaps the chief, bit the boy. The boy died instantly of the venom. At once the Indians stoned that snake, the one that had bitten the boy, but only that one. The others fled back to the hill of Toji-vachaca. Never more did they return anywhere near their town.

The wrinkled storyteller continues. Since that time whenever we, the Guatuso Indians, kill a snake, we cut off the head and stretch the body under the leaves. And on winter nights, when Zi-ije is absent from the sky, we remember the boy—the boy in the clouds who, with his hand of fire, traces serpents of light. And we say, that the snake may not strike us, "Zaálan, Zaálan . . . Talazú!"

NANDAYURE
AND HIS MAGIC ROD

It was said that Nandayure, the *cacique* or chief of Nicoya, possessed a magic rod. With it he could make anything made of lime disappear.

His enemies feared this magic rod, and with reason. Once or twice Nandayure had ruined their pearl fishing for them. He had only to extend the magic rod over the canoes loaded with oyster shells and the pearls, together with the iris-colored shells that harbored them, vanished in vapor. You might say, a day's work gone up in smoke.

Being a just man, Nandayure seldom abused his power, seldom used it, in fact. Only when his subjects were particularly irksome—quarreling, complaining, criticizing. The younger men were most apt to irritate.

They would say, "Really, why we are so bound by old and outworn rules we do not know. We pass our time hunting and fishing and mining gold when we'd rather make war or play ball or snore in our hammocks. Work, work, work. If the *cacique* would wave that wand of his over the cliffs, the stone would vanish and we'd only have to pick up the gold. But no, he says that work develops character or some such nonsense. Really, he is old-fashioned . . . a nice enough old fellow, but behind the times."

However, Nandayure did not let this grumbling upset him. After all, he was the one owning the rod. Moreover, he was the chief.

One night this *cacique*, Nandayure, went to a dance, a dance to which he had been asked by one of the councillors of the tribe. It was not uncommon for Nandayure to be invited to celebrations—but it was most unusual for him to accept the invitation.

Nandayure was a dignified man, proud, serious, stuffy. Oh, not stuffy. Well—occasionally stuffy. In any case, not a partygoer. But this once, as a caprice, he attended a party.

While the couples danced in the open air, their movements interwoven with the leaping flames of the fire, Nandayure chatted with the other guests. Casually he turned to contemplate the dancers. For some reason the women appeared different. What was it . . . ?

With sudden indignation Nandayure discovered that they had covered their faces with the white powder of gypsum. They were hiding the shiny bronze patina of their natural beauty. (This was the way the *cacique* thought. I told you he was sometimes stuffy.)

Nandayure was carried away by his anger. A profanation of tradition! A flouting of natural custom! (He was off again.)

Without considering the consequences of his action, Nandayure stretched his rod toward the dancers. *This* would rid their faces of the cosmetic!

He succeeded. Oh, very well. The cosmetic vanished—a little too well. Those slender and graceful bodies of the women were converted into loose sacks of membrane and muscle and skin. All bones had disappeared. Their partners, the strong warriors of Nicoya, could scarcely hold the bodies in their arms.

Horror paralyzed everyone. The music-makers ceased their drumbeats. Cries of grief and despair echoed through the air. Nandayure himself was overcome with sorrow. What had he done? What possessed him to make such a foolish, thoughtless gesture? He groaned. The young men were right. He was too old, too muddle-headed to be a *cacique.*

He looked down at the rod, the magic rod, the cause of the disaster. Once again Nandayure gave in to his feelings. (After all, it had been an extraordinary evening.) With a movement of repulsion, he hurled the rod as far as he could, into the middle of the fire.

The spectators stared, aghast. Life was becoming too complicated for them. First, the *cacique* dissolved their women, or what held their women together. Secondly, he threw his magic rod, his talisman, his very symbol of power, into the fire. What was the world coming to?

They watched the magic rod change to charred black and then to gray ashes. And when this occurred, when the rod had disappeared—why, the bones reappeared. There were the women, standing firm and shapely once more. Everyone gave a great sigh of relief—especially the men who had been supporting their floppy partners.

Again happiness reigned. Again were heard the drums fashioned of iguana skins. Once more they danced, those strong warriors and the women with powdered faces.

Was Nandayure concerned? Far from it. Tradition says that he was so giddy with joy that he asked the whitest-faced girl to dance with him—and shortly thereafter he overcame his stuffiness sufficiently to marry her.

THE
TREASURE OF NOSARA

The fishermen of Nicoya assure me that in the silent nights of summer, when the moon appears a pale dancer on an immense blue carpet, they frequently hear the wailing and sobbing of a woman. The cries come from the banks of the river. Does this mysterious she search for something lost near the turbulent waters?

No one rushes to find out. No one flies to offer assistance. Goodness, no. Spirits, ghosts, apparitions must fend for themselves. Troubles enough there already are in this world without borrowing those of another.

Some believe the sobs to belong to the Weeping Woman. Others say it is a witch wandering along the river to agitate fishermen. But an old fellow of the area shakes his head. He tells me that in Nicoya neither the Weeping Woman nor witches exist. What *does* exist is a treasure, hidden five hundred years ago by a princess of Nicoya. It is enough to make anyone wail—that is, if he can't find the treasure. What is this treasure? Who secreted it? And why?

The Enchanted Orchard

In the fifteenth century the peninsula of Nicoya was, as it still is, one of the most beautiful and fertile regions of Central America. Through the violet hills, through forests of palms and robust *espabeles,* where the larks sing, flow murmuring rivers. They water the fields of black earth where the ancient inhabitants of Nicoya, the Chorotegas, grew their corn and beans and chilies. They roar past the scarred cliffs where the Chorotegas mined their gold.

Living in this land of plenty, the Chorotegas were a people of warriors. They had to be, to defend their riches from poor and jealous tribes. Around their abundance they had built a well-ordered life of custom and tradition.

One year the *cacique* of Nicoya, a man of ambition, made an announcement. The first of the three annual celebrations in honor of the sun, he said, would this year exceed all former parties in pomp and solemnity. His subjects were delighted. They translated pomp and solemnity into gaiety and merrymaking (which is what the *cacique* had meant in the first place but was too pompous to say so). He sent messengers to invite all his vassals. From near and far the guests poured in. They, too, guessed what pomp and solemnity really meant. Late on a clear August day the festivities began.

Unknown to the Chorotegas, their rivals of many years, the Indians of Chira, were plotting against them. After all, they hadn't been invited to the party—no wonder they were miffed. But they definitely overdid things. Taking advantage of the activities, they planned to fall on the Chorotegas and carry off the golden treasure of the *cacique*. Gaiety and merrymaking they might lack, but gold they were determined to have.

Fifty warriors, traveling in ten canoes under the command of Nacaome, a grim but able Chireño, landed on the coast of the peninsula. It was early on the second day of the celebration.

The Chorotegas, having passed the night in dancing and drinking *chicha*, were unaware of danger. In fact, they were unaware of just about everything. Most were sound asleep. The *cacique* snored peacefully in his hammock. His daughter Nosara was awake only because she was flirting with Curime, a young man of a visiting tribe. And *she* was yawning—but politely pretending that she wasn't.

Suddenly, just as the sun shot its rays down, down the mountains, war whoops and the whistle of arrows proclaimed the enemy attack. There was confusion and terror. The women fled to the forest. The men were muddled and heavy-headed. The *cacique* tried to believe it was a nightmare and turned over—but an arrow in his leg convinced him. He sat up, pained in leg and head.

Nosara, guessing the goal of the Chireños, leaped to her feet. "Come!" she cried to her young man. "We must save my father's treasure." A practical girl, Nosara.

They rushed to the pavilion, where Nosara caught

up the jar containing little figures fashioned of gold—eagles, bees, caimans. Did she ask her father's permission? Did she bid him good-bye? The tale doesn't tell. We know only that with the treasure and a bow and arrow, she and Curime ran into the woods.

Not a moment too soon. The next instant, Nacaome, the leader of the Chireños, entered the *cacique's* home. He searched it thoroughly, under jug and jar, without finding the coveted gold. You can imagine how provoked he was. All those plans, all that distance, and not a nugget to show for them.

In desperation he secured the Chorotegan nobles and threatened them with death if they did not reveal the treasure of Nicoya. They told nothing for a very good reason—they knew nothing.

But the wife of one of the prisoners, in fear for her husband, cried out, "Nosara took it! She carried it with her into the forest." At once Nacaome sent five warriors to follow the girl.

All that day Nosara and Curime made their way through the woods. When night fell, they sank exhausted under the *ojoche* whose fallen flowers made a soft place for them. But a few minutes later they heard the yells of their enemies. Wearily they continued their flight.

During the whole night they ran. The Chireños were good hunters—and accustomed to fatigue and hunger. They never lost the track; they seldom rested. Like the sun they were in their inflexibility.

At dawn Nosara and Curime reached the banks of the river. They looked at each other in despair.

34

"I will hide it," said Nosara. "They may catch us, but they will not find the treasure." Resolute as well as practical, that Nosara.

She ran into the wildness, into the mountain. For a long while Curime waited for her on the bank of the river. Just as she reappeared, the Chireños fell upon them. When the lovers turned to flee, the warriors loosed their arrows on them. Both were killed. A pity for everyone, for search as they might, the Chireños could never find the gold that Nosara had hidden or buried in the mountains.

And to this day, when at night the sad cries are heard from the river, there are Indians who whisper, "Hush! Hush! It is the Princess Nosara. After all these years she has forgotten where the treasure is hidden. She is searching, searching, searching . . ."

THE
LAGOON OF MASAYA

The scientists and intellectuals of Nicaragua maintain that the lovely Lagoon of Masaya is the result of a volcanic eruption. The lake itself rests in the crater of a gigantic volcano.

But . . . indeed not, say the Indians. A respectable opinion worthy of a scholar, but not true—not true at all. We all know it happened another way. What way then? Listen, and we shall tell you.

Years and years ago the region from Monimbó west to Quitapayo and north to the town of Nindirí was covered with thick and beautiful woods and rich meadows. Limiting the forest on the east was a sinuous line of blue mountains. In the valley of these hills, through the woods by diverse roads, the inhabitants of Quitapayo and the neighboring villages of Nimboja and Nandayure would travel to the prosperous town of Nindirí.

One day there appeared in the forest a great serpent with horns. Terrified, the Indians consulted a *brujo*, or soothsayer. After much frowning and nodding and pacing, this one announced that the serpent was beneficial and useful. In order that he might not run away, he should be fastened to the trunk of an elm tree.

This the Indians did. But with greater terror they noted that the serpent easily broke away from the maguey and rattan cords with which he was tied. More worried than ever, they again consulted the *brujo*. It was simply impossible to tie up the reptile. And no fun, either—no fun at all.

The soothsayer responded that they should take some long hairs from the heads of girls twelve to fourteen years old and with these make a rope. Using this rope, they should once more tie the serpent to the tree.

Out of sight of the *brujo*'s hut, the Indians looked at each other with raised eyebrows. They shrugged their shoulders, pursed their lips. Make a worthwhile rope with girls' hair? Obviously the soothsayer was in a joking mood. Too bad *he* wasn't the one to plait the hair and then lasso the serpent with it. Then the laugh would be on somebody else's face . . .

However, the Indians did as they were told. With stupefaction they observed that no matter how violent his efforts to loose himself, the serpent could not break the cord of woven hair.

Once gentled, the serpent laid an egg. After three days the egg cracked, and out of it burst a stream of crystal water. First a pool formed, then a pond, and this stretched on and on and up and up, rising higher and higher against the hills. The people followed the example of the water, climbing higher and higher into the mountains. Finally, there lay the lagoon, clear and ample and deep.

The woods now lay at the bottom of the lake. They still do. And the serpent still lies tied to a tree way, way beneath. On the east, the blue cordillera borders the beautiful lagoon, its peaks and volcanoes reflected in the quiet waters.

And even today the serpent claims his annual tribute. So that the spell of the lagoon does not disappear, three people must drown in these waters every year. This is what the serpent wishes. The people? Well, they are not asked. But the wise stay well away from the lagoon. Look at it, admire it, yes—but swim or paddle in a boat? There are better things to do than please a serpent, even a magic serpent . . .

HOW
THE MOON CAME TO BE

Long ago in the land of Guatemala there was a *cacique* who had a beautiful daughter. The *cacique* loved his daughter so much that he wanted her all to himself. He would allow no one to look at her, not even the sun. Especially not the sun, since he was such a cocky, ambitious fellow.

When the sun learned of this, he decided the girl should be his wife. Nothing but the best for him. Anyway, who was this *cacique* to stand in his way?

One day the father was away in the forest shooting wood pigeons with his blowgun. The sun seized the opportunity and shaded his face with a turtle's shell. Noticing the pleasant shade, the girl went out of doors to enjoy it. As he peeped from behind the shell, the sun saw that she was indeed beautiful. Ay, ay, ay! No time to lose. While she sat in her garden, the sun sent down one of his rays to bring her up to the sky. And with her husband the sun, the girl was very happy.

But the *cacique?* Ah, that was flour from another

sack, as they say. Pacing up and down, up and down, the *cacique* wasted not a glance on the blue mountains, the tall trees, the shining lakes of his kingdom. He had one thought in mind—revenge. Revenge on the sun was a serious matter. It took much pacing and many thoughts to arrive at an idea. Once the idea was caught, the *cacique* put it to use. He summoned the best gunmaker in the land.

"Gunmaker," he said briskly, "I want the longest, largest, and finest blowgun ever made. Spare no pains. Waste no time. The *best* blowgun is what I want."

"To shoot jaguars?" asked the gunmaker with interest.

"Jaguars? Certainly not. The gun is to shoot the sun—the rascal who ran off with my daughter."

The gunmaker, much impressed, set to work. He also set half the village to work. A dozen men were sent to cut down the most enormous stalk of the most enormous *pubché* tree and tow it to the village. The gunmaker cleaned the pulp from inside the stalk.

"Sandpaper bark. Where is the sandpaper bark? Haven't those scamps returned yet? At their age I could have made ten round trips and . . ." Just then the boys ran in with the bark from the sandpaper tree.

The gunmaker put all the women and all the children of the village to work rubbing the *pubché* stalk with the sandpaper bark. "Smooth and shiny as the lake it must be," he told them. "It will be the gun of guns. To shoot the sun, no less. If you ask me, the *cacique* is overreaching himself. Jaguars, tapirs, croco-

diles, well and good. But the sun? What will he do
with it when he shoots it? Well, thanks to the gods, it's
not my problem."

When the stalk was smoothed inside and out until
it felt and shone like polished gold, it was set aside to
season. Meanwhile, the shotmakers were forming balls
of clay—tremendous balls that took five strong men to
lift. And inside his palace the *cacique* was gulping in
great breaths of air and storing them away in his lungs.
He would need quite a number to send one of those
balls to the sun.

At last the gunmaker announced the gun was
ready. The weavers of the village wove a net of bark
around it. The ropemakers twined and plaited vines
into strong ropes. With these, the village men hauled
the great gun through the fragrant forests, past the
glimmering lakes, up the blue hills to the highest
mountaintop. Then they went back to drag up the
heavy balls of clay. And finally they carried up the *cacique* so he wouldn't lose any of his breath climbing by
himself.

All the villagers gathered around. It was the most
exciting occasion of their lives. Being fond of the *cacique,* they wanted him to hit the sun, but still. . . .
What if the sun were hurt so badly that he fell out of
the sky? That couldn't bear thinking about. So they
hoped with all their might that the *cacique* might hit
the sun . . . but only a nick, just enough to show him
he shouldn't go stealing people's daughters.

The shotmakers loaded the gun. The *cacique*,

swollen to twice his size with the stored-up breath, put his lips on the gun. He drew in one last deep breath and . . . fell into a fit of coughing. The sun had thrown a handful of red pepper down the muzzle of the gun. The *cacique* and his subjects coughed and coughed and coughed. And this, it is said, was the beginning of whooping cough in Guatemala.

It took some time for the *cacique* to get rid of his cough. And it took more time to recapture all the breaths he'd lost. Finally the *cacique* was ready again. He curled his lips around the gun. Again the sun threw down a handful of red pepper . . . with no effect. One can have whooping cough only once.

With his hundreds of breaths the *cacique* blew. Oh yes, the ball hit the sun—not so hard as to knock him down, but hard enough so that he dropped the *cacique*'s daughter. She, poor girl, fell into the ocean and broke to pieces.

Each of the pieces wept and cried to be taken back to the sun. How they carried on! The little silver fish of the sea were disturbed by all this wailing. Moreover, they felt sorry for the girl. None of this was *her* doing.

They gathered up all the pieces. Then, using salt from the sea and their own silver scales, they patched her together again. Not in the same shape, perhaps— but still beautiful. Now, how to get her back to the sun?

One of the fish had an idea. "Let's all catch hold of each other's tails. Then we'll weave ourselves into a

mat. That way we can all jump together and carry the girl up to her husband."

That is what they did. The plan nearly worked. The thousands of silver fish matted themselves under the mended girl and leaped for the sun. They were not quite strong enough to reach it, but at least they managed to stick the girl in the sky. They themselves were stuck, too—forever. They remained in the sky as the Milky Way.

As for the girl—you can see her, patched up but in one piece, riding high in the sky. She is the moon, and she spends her time following the sun, hoping one day to catch up with him. Sometimes she nearly does, and they slide down the western horizon, one right behind the other.

The sun looks back and almost waits for her . . . but then he remembers the birds huddled in feathery sleep on the other side of the world, and he thinks, what will they do without me? Dream for another hour? That would never do. So he goes on his way.

THE
BEGINNING OF MAIZE

Did you know that the first corn was developed in the highlands of Guatemala and southern Mexico? While this grain has spread throughout the world, its close relative the *teosinte* grass is still found only in these two countries. Today the Indians tell this story of maize and *teosinte*.

Once, long ago, a god, Bitol, and his goddess wife, Tzacol, were resting in a forest. To them came the jaguar, the coyote, the eagle, and the parrot. "Good day to you," said their spokesman the parrot, bobbing his yellow head. "If you will come with us, we have something of value to show you."

Now Bitol and Tzacol were somewhat suspicious. They knew the coyote and parrot to be mischief-makers, while the jaguar and eagle were sometimes on one side, sometimes the other. In other words, undependable. However, curiosity overcame caution, and the two gods followed the wild creatures.

On reaching a prairie divided by a wide river, the

parrot waved his wing. "Look you. As you see, we were not joking."

There on the bank lay a laughing baby boy. He was neither human nor god, for his mother was a wave of the river and his father a beam of sunlight. Whatever he was, he was beautiful. Tzacol could not resist him. She persuaded Bitol that she must have him, and she carried him home with her to raise with her other children. The gods gave him the name of Teosinte.

Teosinte grew into a handsome youth, slim and tall and straight, with soft auburn hair. To the dismay of Bitol and Tzacol, he fell in love with his youngest foster sister Ma-ix. No wonder! A lovely girl, slim and tall and straight, with dark eyes and pearly teeth and soft auburn hair.

You might have thought the old couple would be delighted. Far from it. In some ways gods and mortals are much alike.

"He shall not marry her," they protested. "He is no god. Not even a human. Beautiful, yes. But so is a butterfly, or a hummingbird. Pay him no heed, Ma-ix. We will find for you a god worthy to be your husband."

Coax and warn and scold as they might, it did no good. Not only was Teosinte madly in love with Ma-ix; more importantly, she loved no one but him.

Bitol and Tzacol should have known enough to give in gracefully—or at least to give in. But no, they nagged the two, on and on and on. They pointed out attractive girls to Teosinte. They whispered to Ma-ix the charms of the eligible young gods.

One morning they awoke to find Ma-ix and Teo-sinte gone. It was a surprise to no one but Bitol and Tzacol. The old couple was thunderstruck.

"We'll feed him to the god of fire!" cried Bitol.

"We'll give him back to his mother the river," said Tzacol. "With his hands and feet bound so this time he'll be obliged to stay with her."

But they put off the time for carrying out their threats. Secretly they hoped for the return of the two. They might . . . they just might . . . with remorse and affection be persuaded to forgive and bestow their blessing.

As months passed and the young couple did not appear, Bitol and Tzacol grew anxious. This was carrying things too far. No affection. No remorse. No return. They set out for the prairie and stream where they had first found Teosinte.

On the bank, no Ma-ix, no Teosinte. There was nobody at all—only two plants growing side by side. Both were tall and slim and straight, and both had soft auburn hair. Both had leaf-wrapped ears. While those of one plant had small, withered grains, those of the other had grains white and pearly as the teeth of Ma-ix.

The plant with the small kernels was left to grow as it would. "That is the spirit of Teosinte," said the two gods. "He stole our daughter. He shall have no welcome from us. Back to the wilds for him."

The more beautiful and graceful plant they took with them. They named it Maiz for their daughter, and they tended it carefully so that future ears should grow in size and tenderness and beauty. Thus maize or corn came into the world.

And the poor weed *teosinte* grows uncared for through the plateaus of Guatemala. The Indians pass it by and sigh, "Ah, Teosinte, now you know—one does not defy the gods and escape unpunished."

THE
FIRST FLUTE

During the glory of the Mayan civilization, years before the coming of the Spanish, there lived a *cacique* who had a beautiful daughter, the Princess Nima-Cux, whom he loved dearly.

Not only was Nima-Cux beautiful, she was possessed of talents. She could plait grass into fine baskets. She could mold little animals out of clay—and you even knew exactly which animals they were supposed to be. The coati had a long ringed tail. The puma had an open mouth showing sharp teeth. The tapir's snout was definitely snoutish. The snake wound round and round and round—and if you unwound him, he reached from Nima-Cux's toes to her earplugs.

Above all, Nima-Cux could sing like a bird. Her voice tripped up and down the scale as easily as her feet tripped up and down the steps. The *cacique* sat back and counted his blessings. They all had to do with Nima-Cux, her beauty, her baskets, her clay work, and, especially, her voice.

As princesses should, Nima-Cux had everything she asked for—besides some things she hadn't thought of requesting. There were finely carved dolls, necklaces of rare shells, a cape of bright parrot feathers, an enormous garden filled with flowers and blossoming trees and singing birds and pet animals. No wonder Nima-Cux was happy.

Thus life flowed along, contentedly for everyone in the household until Nima-Cux neared her sixteenth birthday. Suddenly she became sad and melancholy. Nothing made her happy. Then again, nothing made her unhappy. She just *was*, for no reason at all, she said.

The *cacique* was greatly agitated. He strode up and down the garden, wondering, wondering what would please Nima-Cux. Another doll? A bright fish? A golden plate for her breast-of-pheasant? But to whatever he proposed, Nima-Cux would only murmur politely, "No. But thank you, Papa."

The cook sent boys scampering up the tallest palm trees to bring back heart of palm for Nima-Cux's dinner.

Hunters were ordered into the jungle to capture monkeys. "Mind you, *funny* monkeys to entertain the princess. Not a sad one in the crowd—or off comes your head."

Maidens roamed the royal gardens gathering orchids to ornament the princess' bedchamber.

What happened? Nima-Cux would peer at the rare *palmito* and moan softly, "I am not hungry."

She would stare at the monkeys cavorting on the branches while the royal household screamed in amusement and whisper, "Yes, yes, very comical," and sigh deeply. The household would hush its laughter and echo her sighs.

The orchids went unnoticed until they dropped to the floor with a dry rustle.

Herb doctors came. Witch doctors came. Old hunched crones said to know the secrets of life came. They all said, "But she seems quite well and normal. A bit pale. A trifle listless. Perhaps a good tonic . . ."

Nima-Cux was annoyed enough to argue about the tonic. "That smelly stuff? I won't even taste it."

Finally a sorcerer somewhat wiser than the others spoke to the *cacique*. "After all, the princess is practically sixteen. Other girls her age are married. Find a good husband for the Princess Nima-Cux—and she will again shine radiant as a star."

The *cacique* shook his head. A *husband?* How could a mere husband bring her happiness if her own father could not? A poor suggestion. What were sorcerers coming to?

He peeked once more at Nima-Cux's dismal face —and in desperation sent messengers throughout his kingdom. The young man skillful enough to impress the princess and coax a smile to her lips would become her husband. In a week the first tournament would be held.

During the next week the roads were worn into holes by the thousands of footsteps. Everyone in the kingdom hurried to the palace either to take part or to watch the take-parters (or is it takers-part?). Seats were constructed for the nobility. Those not so noble found a patch of thick grass, a loop of vine, or a high branch. The *cacique* and Nima-Cux sat on a canopied stand. The tournaments began.

The first contestant marched out proud and arrogant in his gold tunic, attended by a troop of warriors. A handsome youth he was. Maidens fainted with joy at the sight of him. The rest of the contestants growled and trembled.

But Nima-Cux frowned and asked, "What can he *do?* Besides prance and preen, worse than any *quetzal?*"

The *cacique* sighed and made a sign for the warrior to display his talents—if any. The soldiers stood before the young man and threw ears of corn into the air. With his bow and arrows the warrior shot kernels from the ears in regimental procession. One row, then the next and next until all the kernels were gone.

The spectators cheered and shouted with admiration. Such skill—and such elegance! Ayyyyyyy! The other contestants ground their teeth and sobbed.

Nima-Cux yawned and asked politely, "May we see the second match, Papa? The first has taken up *so* much time."

The *cacique* sighed again and motioned for the tournament to continue.

The second competitor strode out as confident and proud as the first. He walked alone, bearing a large basket. When he set it down, out slithered a tremendous snake of a poisonous variety, its eyes glaring with malevolence.

The spectators gasped with horror. Maidens fainted with fear. The remaining rivals watched with relish.

The youth engaged the angry snake in combat, artfully evading its deadly fangs. The spectators held their breaths.

"How boring!" muttered Nima-Cux, staring into the distance.

"Really? Really, daughter? You don't like it?" asked the *cacique* with regret. (He was enjoying the contests immensely.)

He motioned for more action. The youth complied by squeezing the life from the snake. Then he bowed to the applause of the crowd. Or most of the crowd. Nima-Cux was already on her way to the palace and her couch with a headache.

For days the tournaments continued. The most handsome and courageous of the Mayan youth competed with each other for the favor of Nima-Cux— favor that was nowhere to be seen. Certainly not on her lips, which remained clamped in a sulky line. Nor in her eyes, which gazed sadly at the competition without seeing it.

Finally the last contestant appeared, a merry boy wearing the tattered dress of a minstrel. The spectators smiled. The other contestants laughed scornfully. With a quick bow to the princess, the boy began to sing. He sang of the lakes, the forests, the hills of the highlands. He sang of the crystal stars flashing from the dark river of night. He sang of love.

Not bad, not bad, nodded the *cacique*. Not, of course, to compare with Nima-Cux's singing. He glanced at his daughter. What astonishment! Her eyes resembled the crystal of the song. Her lips were open and curving—upward. She was smiling! The *cacique* sat back and pondered the puzzle of life and love.

"I like him, Papa. We can sing together. I will marry him. Only first, he must learn the song of each bird of the forest. Then he can teach me."

The minstrel was happy to oblige. He had *meant* it when he sang of love. At once he disappeared into the jungle.

Day after day he practiced, imitating this bird, then that one. But Guatemala is home to hundreds, thousands of birds. Some whistle a complicated tune. The minstrel began to despair of his task.

The god of the forest, after listening for days to the young minstrel's efforts, took pity on him. Also on the birds and other wild inhabitants of the woods—not to mention himself. He appeared before the minstrel, wearing a kindly smile.

"Perhaps I can help you," he offered. "It is a difficult exercise you are engaged in."

Severing a small limb from a tree, the god removed the pith and cut a series of holes in the tube. "Now attend carefully," he said. And he instructed the young man exactly how to blow into one end while moving his fingers over the holes. The notes of the birds tumbled out, clear and sweet.

With a torrent of thanks, the minstrel flew on his way, carrying the *chirimia,* or flute. Just in time. Nima-Cux, anxious that the chore she had assigned her lover had been impossible, was on the point of another decline. She received the youth with joy. Enchanted she was with the flute and its airs . . . with the minstrel and his airs.

The two were married and lived long and happily in the palace of the *cacique.* And today the Indians of Guatemala will point to the *chirimia,* the most typical of native instruments, and tell you this is the way it came about.

THE
CREATION OF MAN

The *Popol Vuh,* the sacred book of the ancient Quiché Maya Indians of Guatemala, tells the story of the creation of man.

Three times the Creator formed man, of three different materials. Twice He was dissatisfied with His work.

The first men He created were of clay. But they were soft and weak. They could not move. In the first rain they melted into nothing. So the Creator broke them up and threw them away.

The second time the Creator, called the Heart of Heaven, formed men of wood. He peopled the earth with these wooden figures. But the figures had no minds, no souls. They had no thoughts, no feelings, no strength. Moreover, these beings never spoke to their Creator, never praised Him, never remembered Him, never gave a thought to Him. For that reason the Creator resolved to destroy the wooden figures.

He sent down the eagle Xecotcovach to peck out

their eyes. The great vampire bat Camalotz flew down to snip off their heads. Cotzbalam, the tiger, was there to devour their flesh. And finally came the tapir Tucumbalam to break and mangle their bones. This was to punish the wooden figures for not remembering their Creator, the Heart of Heaven.

To punish them further, the Heart of Heaven darkened the face of earth and sent a black rain, a rain by day and a rain by night. And there came small animals and large animals, and sticks and stones, to strike the faces of the wooden figures. And their jars, their bowls, their plates, their pots, their dogs-that-did-not-bark, their grinding stones—all these which had always been silent—came suddenly to have tongues and to speak.

"Much evil you did unto us. You devoured us. Now we will eat you," said the domestic birds, the turkey, the pheasant, the wild hen.

The grinding stones cried, "You tormented us. Each day, every day, every night, every dawn, you crushed our faces against the grain and the stone. Because of you our faces cried HOLI, HOLI, HUQUI, HUQUI. That was the tribute we paid you. But now that you have stopped being men, you shall feel our strength. We will grind and reduce your flesh to dust." Thus cried the grinding stones.

And the dogs-that-did-not-bark whined and said, "Why would you not feed us? We were only watching, and you chased us and drove us away. Always you kept a stick ready to strike us as you were eating. This is how you treated us. We could not speak to complain. But now we will destroy you; now you shall feel the teeth of our mouths. Now we will devour you." Thus whined the dogs-that-did-not-bark, and they destroyed the faces of the wooden figures.

And their jars, their *comales,* their plates, their pots spoke to them. "Grief and suffering you caused us. Our mouths and our faces were begrimed with soot. We were placed over the fire. You burned us as if we could feel no pain. Now we will burn you." Thus spoke the pots.

The stones of the hearth, which were placed one above the other, all hurled themselves from their places against the heads of the wooden men to make them suffer.

As fast as they could, they ran, the desperate wooden men. They climbed on top of the houses, but the houses fell, throwing the wooden figures to the ground. They climbed trees, and the trees hurled them far. They wished to enter caves, and the caves repelled them.

Thus was the destruction of the men who had been created. The wooden figures were destroyed, their mouths and their faces destroyed. Only a few escaped.

It is said that the descendents of these few are the monkeys which exist now in the forests. These are the remnant of those men, those wooden men made by the Creator.

For this reason the monkey resembles man. He is

the sample of a generation of men created, of men who were only puppets and made only of wood.

Then for a long, long time the Heart of Heaven and the other Creators held counsel. They thought about what material should next be used to create mankind.

There came to the Creators four creatures, the mountain cat, the coyote, the parrot, and the crow, with word of corn, the yellow ears and the white ears. They showed the Creators the road to the places of Paxil and Cayalá.

The Creators were overjoyed at finding a beautiful land, abundant in yellow corn and white corn, *cacao*, fruit and honey. They knew now what they must do. Four men they created. Four men were formed by the Creators of dough of cornmeal.

They were well-formed and handsome men. They could see and hear and walk and converse. They could see all that was around them and all that was hidden from them. They could see into the forests, the rocks, the lakes, the seas, the mountains, and the valleys. So intelligent were they, they knew all there was to know in the world.

The Creators asked the four men, "Can you see? Can you hear? Can you walk and talk? Look then at the world. Can you see the forests and the lakes and the mountains and the valleys?"

The men were quick to see all that was in the world. And they answered the Creators, "We see and hear, we think and feel, we move and walk. We see all in the arch of the sky and all on the round face of the earth. We know all. We give you thanks, two and three times, O Creators, for our creation, for giving us being."

But the Creators were not pleased with this speech. Again they took counsel and contemplated their work.

And they said, "Are these men not the creatures of our making? Must they also be gods? Must they be the equals of their Creators and see all and know all? Let them see only that which is near. Let them know only that which they see."

Then the Creator, the Heart of Heaven, blew a mist over their eyes so they could see only as in a fog. No longer could they see all and know all, but only that which was close to them. So the wisdom and the knowledge that the four men were created with were destroyed.

In this way were the first men, the fathers of the world, formed by the Creator, the Heart of Heaven.

THE
TRICKS OF HUNAHPÚ
AND IXBALANQUÉ

The mischievous boy-gods Hunahpú and Ixbalanqué set themselves to do some work—not for the
sake of work, but to gain the favor of their mother and
grandmother.

"We go to plant a cornfield," they said. "Do not
worry about us, Mother and Grandmother. We will
work hard. But at midday bring us food, for we shall
be hungry."

"Very well. At midday I shall come with food," answered their grandmother. "Work hard, my grandsons."

The boys left, carrying axes and picks and hoes
and their blowguns. Soon they came to a flat piece of
forest. "This will do," they said.

With one stroke they sank the ax into the trunk of
a tree. Then the ax went on alone to do its work. It
hacked and it hewed until all the trees and branches
were lying on the ground.

With another stroke the boys plunged the pick

into the wildness. The pick continued its work alone. It dug and it cleaned until all the brush and vines and brambles lay in heaps on the ground.

With a third stroke, they set the hoe into the earth. Alone it went on with its work. It scraped and it loosened and it leveled till the earth was as soft as feathers.

While all this work was being done, Hunahpú and Ixbalanqué caught and tamed a turtledove called Xmucur. They sent the dove to the top of a tall tree and said, "Watch for our grandmother, who comes bringing food. When you see her, begin at once to sing. Then we will know to take up the pick and the ax."

The boys went off to amuse themselves with their blowguns. They shot buds from the tree limbs. They shot a berry from the mouth of a mouse. They shot a straw from the beak of a sora. They bothered themselves not at all with the chopping and the clearing and the cultivating.

After a little, hearing the dove sing, they ran and snatched up the ax and the pick. Hunahpú took earth and smeared his head and hands with it so that he looked like a true laborer. Ixbalanqué threw chips of wood over his hair and shoulders to resemble a true woodsman.

"Well, I see you have been working," said their grandmother, impressed with their warm appearance.

Without a word the mischievous boys took the food and ate it at once. All their playing with blowguns had made them hungry. When their grandmother

63

had gone, they stretched themselves under a tree for a nap. When they awoke, they went home. They made themselves appear so weary that their mother and grandmother felt sorry for them.

"Tomorrow do not work so hard," they said, setting a good meal before them. Hunahpú and Ixbalanqué ate heartily as if they had spent the day laboring. Then they went to sleep.

The next day when they returned to the place with their axes, their picks, their hoes, and their blowguns, they found no field. The trees and the brush stood as before, and the vines and brambles had enlaced themselves together as tightly as basketwork.

"It is a trick!" the boys cried. "But who could have played it? Perhaps the creatures of the wood did it, the mountain lion, the jaguar, the deer, the rabbit, the wildcat, the coyote, the boar, the coati, and all the birds, large and small. Surely it is those who did it. And in one night they did it."

Once again Hunahpú and Ixbalanqué put the ax and pick and hoe to work. But instead of playing with their blowguns, they sat down to consider.

"How can we keep this from happening again?" they asked. And they decided they must keep watch over the field that night. In that way they would surprise anyone who came to undo their work. *Their* work? Well, let us say, the work of the ax, the pick, and the hoe.

"Can you imagine that, Mother and Grandmother?" they asked when they arrived home. "Here someone has played a joke on us after all our work. Somebody turned our cornfield back into a thick woods filled with brush and brambles. What do you think of that, Mother and Grandmother? But do not be troubled. We have made it into a field again, and we shall watch tonight. That was a bad joke, and we do not want it to happen again."

So that night they returned to their field and wrapped themselves in the darkness.

At midnight they heard a scratching and a scurrying, which came closer and closer. They heard the animals say in their own language, "Rise up, trees! Rise up, vines!" And the trees and the brush and the vines stood as before.

In the blackness Hunahpú and Ixbalanqué saw first the forms of the mountain lion and the jaguar. The boys lunged to catch them, but the mountain lion and the jaguar escaped. The other animals, the wildcat, the coyote, the boar, and the coati, ran, too, and got away. The boys could catch only the tails of the rabbit and the deer, and these came off in their hands. The rabbit and the deer escaped, but to this day these two have short tails.

The boys were angry because they could not seize the animals and punish them. But there came hopping one more animal, the rat, who had lagged behind the others. The boys took him and squeezed him and tried to choke him. They burned his tail in the fire, and for that reason the rat's tail has never since had hair on it.

The rat managed to gasp, "I do not wish to die at

your hands, boys. Besides, it was not of your business
to plant the cornfield."

"And why not? asked the boys.

"Turn me loose a moment and I will tell you. But
first give me something to eat."

"Not until you tell us," answered the boys.

"Very well," said the rat. "The cornfield is not your business. You have other things to do. Did you know that the rubber ball and the ring and gloves of your father and his brother, Hun-Hunahpú and Vucub-Hunahpú, those who died in Xibalbá, hang from the rafters of your home? Your grandmother and mother will not show them to you. They will not tell you of them, for it was on their account that your father and uncle died."

"Ah, ah, is this true?" cried the boys, their hearts happy to learn of the rubber ball. Now that the rat had spoken, they showed him his food, which was the same as their own, and said, "This shall be your food: corn, chili seeds, beans, *cacao*. All these belong to you, and any food that is stored away and forgotten, that is yours also. Now eat. Then let us go, for you must help us."

"But what if your grandmother sees me? What shall I say?" asked the rat.

"Do not trouble yourself about our grandmother. We will see to her. You have only to climb to the rafters and hide yourself."

The next day at noon the boys returned home, bringing the rat with them. While Hunahpú walked boldly into the house, Ixbalanqué crept to the corner of the house and set the rat there to climb. Then he, too, entered the house.

"Grandmother, for lunch we wish corn cakes with chili sauce," they said. Obligingly the grandmother prepared that for them.

Deliberately spilling the contents of the water jug, they cried, "Ah, ah, what have we done? We are dying of thirst and there remains no water."

"Well, well, I will get some," said the grandmother, and she went off to the river carrying the water jug.

The boys began to eat, although they were not really hungry; they only pretended to be in order to deceive their mother. In the reflection of their shiny red chili sauce they watched the rat crawling over the rafters to where the ball and ring and gloves were hanging. Hunahpú sent a *xan*, which is like a mosquito, to puncture the grandmother's water jug. By the river stood the grandmother, trying to stop the water from pouring out.

"Where is Grandmother? What can have happened to her?" the boys cried to their mother. "Our mouths are parched for lack of water."

"I will see what is the matter," said their mother and went down to the river.

As soon as she was gone, the rat gnawed through the cord tied to the ball and ring and gloves. All fell to the ground. The boys gathered them up and hurriedly hid them near the road leading to the ball court. Then they raced down to the river.

"What has happened? We thought you would never come," they called.

There their mother and grandmother were taking turns holding their fingers over the hole. But nothing helped. The water still spurted forth.

68

"Here, let us fix it," Ixbalanqué said in a superior way. The boys fastened a blob of resin to the hole so that the water stopped at once.

They all returned to the house, the mother and grandmother slowly and with care, the boys leaping and laughing.

THE MESSAGE

Very happily the boy-gods Hunahpú and Ixbalanqué ran off to the ball court to play ball. They cleaned the court, where their father and uncle before them had played, and played by themselves for a long time.

Hearing them, the gods of the underworld, the lords of Xibalbá, asked each other, "Who are those who play over our heads and annoy us with their racket? Can it be they have returned from the dead, Hun-Hunahpú and Vucub-Hunahpú, those who swelled themselves with importance before us? Summon them at once!"

The lords called their messengers and told them, "Say to them to come, the lords have commanded. We wish to play ball with them; inside of seven days we wish to play. Tell them that thus have the lords spoken."

The messengers took the wide road that led to the

boys' home. They arrived and found the grandmother, who was eating.

"They must come without fail, so say the lords of Xibalbá," the messengers told the grandmother. "The lords expect them inside of seven days."

"Very well, messengers, they will come," promised the grandmother. And the messengers turned and went back from where they had come.

Then the old woman's heart was filled with anguish. Whom shall I send to fetch my grandsons? Was it not in this same manner that the messengers of Xibalbá came before when they carried off my sons? Sorrowfully she entered her house.

And then she found on her skirt a louse. She placed it in the palm of her hand and watched it move about.

"Little one, would you like to run an errand for me? Would you go to call my grandsons? Tell them I sent you. Tell them messengers were here from the lords of Xibalbá. Inside of seven days my grandsons must go there to play ball with the lords."

Off strutted the louse. On the way he found one called Tamazul, the toad.

"Where are you off to?" the toad asked.

"I go to find the boys. I have a message for them," answered the louse.

"Good, good, but I see how slowly you go. Do you not want me to swallow you? Then you will see how fast I run and we will be there in no time."

"Very well then," answered the louse. So the toad

swallowed him and went on his way, but at a pace more leisurely than rapid. Soon he came upon a large snake named Zaquicaz.

"Where are you going, young Tamazul?" asked the snake.

"I go as messenger. I carry a message in my stomach."

"I see that you are in no hurry. I would arrive much more quickly. Come then!" And he opened his mouth and swallowed Tamazul. And from that time on, the toad has always been the food of snakes.

The snake wiggled along his way until he was seen by a hawk. The hawk swooped down and swallowed him. Thus, to this day the food of hawks is the snake.

The hawk came to the ball court where Hunahpú and Ixbalanqué were playing ball. Perching on a post, he cawed in his hoarse voice, "Vac-có! Vac-có! Here is the hawk!"

"Who is calling? Let us find our blowguns!" cried the boys. And they shot at the eye of the hawk, sending him twirling to the ground. They picked him up and asked, "Why are you here?"

"I bring a message in my stomach. First, cure my eye and then I will give it to you."

The boys picked a bit of rubber from their ball and pressed it against the hawk's eye. *Lotzquic* they called this medicine, and at once it cured the eye perfectly.

"Speak," the boys said.

The Message

The snake Zaquicaz slid from the hawk's beak.

"Say you," the boys ordered the snake.

"Wait," answered the snake. From his mouth hopped the toad.

"What is the message?" the boys asked Tamazul.

"Here you have it," answered the toad and opened his mouth. But nothing came out.

"You lie to us!" the boys said angrily and kicked the toad. Again and again the toad opened wide his mouth, but nothing appeared.

The boys looked into his mouth; there was the louse stuck to a tooth. All the time he had hidden in the toad's mouth and had not been swallowed. Thus the toad was made fun of; moreover, it was not learned what he took as food. He could never run swiftly, and he remained forever the food of snakes.

"Tell us what you have to say," the boys demanded sternly.

The louse answered, "Your grandmother spoke to me so: Go and call my grandsons. Messengers from the lords of Xibalbá came bringing word that you are to play ball with them. You are to bring the ball, the rings, the gloves, and you are to come within seven days. This your grandmother said to me. And she weeps and grieves, and for that reason I have come to you."

"Is this thing true?" the boys asked each other and ran at once to the side of their grandmother. They ran to say good-by to her.

"We are going now, Grandmother. We came only

to tell you farewell. But we will leave you a sign of our fate. We shall each plant a reed in the center of our house. If they dry up, you will know we are dead. 'They are dead!' you will say if the reeds dry up. But if they sprout, 'Ah, they are alive!' you will cry. And you, Mother, do not weep."

And Hunahpú and Ixbalanqué each planted a reed. They planted them inside the house, not in the field, not in moist earth nor in dry earth. In the middle of the house they left the reeds planted.

THE REVENGE

Then off marched Hunahpú and Ixbalanqué, each carrying his blowgun, along with the ball and ring and gloves, and went downward in the direction of Xibalbá, the city of the gods. Here they discovered that the invitation to play ball was only a pretext of the gods to test and destroy the boy-gods. And many tests there were, but never could the gods conquer Hunahpú and Ixbalanqué. They were not conquered, even when their bones were ground to powder and thrown into the river, and the gods rejoiced, thinking at last that the boys were defeated. But they were not.

The following day Hunahpú and Ixbalanqué presented themselves disguised as two poor boys, with old faces and miserable aspect, dressed in rags; their appearance was hardly one for rejoicing. Thus they were seen by those of Xibalbá.

And what they did was a little enough thing (to them). They occupied themselves in dancing the dance of *Puhuy*, the owl, of *Cux*, the weasel, and the dance of *Iboy*, the armadillo. They danced also the dance of *Ixtzul*, the centipede, and of *Chitic*, the dance of him who walks on stilts.

Moreover, they worked numerous marvels. They seemed to set fire to houses so that they flamed; then they made them return to their former state unharmed. Many of those of Xibalbá viewed all this with admiration.

In addition, the two cut one another to pieces; they killed each other. One would appear quite dead, and then he would revive. This would then happen to the other. Those of Xibalbá watched with amazement all the boys did; and this was the beginning of Hunahpú's and Ixbalanqué's triumph over those of Xibalbá.

The notice of their dances came to the ears of the gods, the *Señores* Hun-Camé and Vucub-Camé. On hearing it, they exclaimed, "Who are those two orphans? Do they really entertain so well?"

"Certainly their dances are very beautiful, and so is all that they do," replied the one who had brought the news.

Satisfied with this, the lords sent their messengers to the boys with great flattery. "Come then, come that we may see what you perform, that we may admire and marvel at you. Thus speak the gods."

So the messengers gave the message and communicated to them the order of the gods, the *Señores*.

"We do not wish to go," the ragged ones answered, "because frankly we are timid. Would we not be ashamed to present ourselves in the house of the gods with our poor countenance, our large eyes, our sad appearance? Do you not see that we are no more than two poor dancers? What will we say to our companions in poverty who have accompanied us and wish to watch our dances and amuse themselves? Could we by chance do the same with the *Señores?* No, no, we do not wish to go, messengers."

In the end they went, their faces weary with vexation and pain. But for a time they dragged their feet so that the messengers had to strike them several times in the face. And thus they journeyed to the residence of the gods.

They arrived before the lords with a meek air. They inclined their heads; then they prostrated themselves, bowing and humbling themselves. They appeared emaciated and tattered, and their aspect was that of vagabonds.

They were asked, "What is your country? What is your town? And who are your father and mother?"

"From where do you come?" they were asked.

"We do not know, *Señor*. We know not the face of our mother nor that of our father. We were small when they died." Thus they answered and spoke no word more.

"Very well. Now perform your tricks that we may admire you. What would you like? We will reward you."

"We do not wish a gift. But truly we are very afraid," they answered the lord.

"Be not afraid. Have no fear. Dance! And perform

the part in which you kill each other. Burn my house. Do what you can do. We will admire you, for that is what our hearts desire. And that you may depart happy, poor boys, we will reward you," the gods told them.

Then the boys began their songs and their dances. All those of Xibalbá came and stood together to see them. They presented the dance of *Cux* and the dance of *Puhuy* and that of *Iboy*.

And the *Señor* said, "Slaughter my dog and then revive him."

"Very well," they said, and they killed the dog. At once they revived him. Truly full of happiness was the dog when he returned to life and wagged his tail when they restored him.

Then the god commanded them, "Burn now my house!" Thus he spoke. And instantly they burned the house of the *Señor*, and although all the lords were together inside the house, they were not burned. At once the house of Hun-Camé was whole again. But immediately it was again in flames.

All the gods marveled, and they were pleased, too, by the dances.

Then the boys were ordered by the *Señor*, "Kill a man and sacrifice him, but do not let him die."

"Very well," these answered. And seizing a man, they slew him and sacrificed him, pulling out his heart and holding it high and then giving it to the view of the lords.

Once more Hun-Camé and Vucub-Camé were astonished. A moment later the man was revived by the boys, and his spirits were happy when he returned to life.

The *Señores* were truly amazed. "Now sacrifice yourselves that we may see this! Our hearts greatly desire to see your performance!" said the gods.

So they sacrificed each other. Hunahpú was sacrificed by Ixbalanqué: one by one his arms and legs were lopped off, his head was cut off and carried to a distance, his heart was snatched from his chest and flung on the grass. All the gods of Xibalbá were fascinated. They watched with admiration to see only one boy dancing and that was Ixbalanqué.

"Rise up!" said this one, and at those words the other returned to life. The boys rejoiced, and the lords also. What was done cheered the hearts of Hun-Camé and Vucub-Camé so that these felt as if they themselves were dancing. Their hearts were filled with desire and anxiety by the dances of the boys.

Then the chief gods, Hun-Camé and Vucub-Camé, gave commands: "Do the same with us! Sacrifice us! Cut us to pieces, one by one!" Thus ordered the lords.

"Very well. Afterwards you will revive. Did you not by chance have us brought here to amuse you, the *Señores*, and your sons and vassals?" they asked the gods.

And first they sacrificed him, the chief of the gods, he who was called Hun-Camé, king of Xibalbá. And when he was dead, they did the same to Vucub-Camé.

And they did not revive them. They did not return them to life.

And when the others saw the *Señores* dead and sacrificed, those of Xibalbá fled from there, for in one moment the two gods were killed and sacrificed. This was done to punish them. Quickly died the two chief gods. And they were not revived.

All the sons and vassals of Xibalbá fled to a great ravine and congregated on a high precipice. There they were gathered when there arrived innumerable ants that discovered them and drove them from the ravine. In this manner they reached a road, and once there they prostrated themselves and delivered themselves, humbled themselves and were much grieved.

Thus were conquered the gods of Xibalbá. Only by magic and through their disguise were Hunahpú and Ixbalanqué able to realize this.

THE
MISSION ENDED

Hunahpú and Ixbalanqué spoke to those of Xibalbá: "Since your great power and your lineage no longer exist and since you deserve little mercy, your prestige will be lowered. Not for you will be the game of *pelota*, the ball game of nobility. Your occupation will be to fashion pots and jars and stones for grinding corn. Only the sons of the desert and the thickets will speak with you. The sons of the dawn, the civilized peoples, will not dwell among you and will flee from your presence. The sinners, the ill-doers, the sad, the wretched, those abandoned to vice, these will take shelter with you. No longer will you govern men, and you will never forget the disgrace of your blood." Thus spoke Hunahpú and Ixbalanqué to all those of Xibalbá.

In the meantime, the grandmother wept and grieved before the reeds they had planted in her house. The reeds sprouted. Then, when the boys were thrown into the oven, they dried up. After, they again sprouted. The grandmother kindled the fire and

burned copal before the reeds in memory of her grandsons. And the grandmother's heart was filled with joy
when the reeds sprouted for the second time. And from
that day, because in the middle of the house were
planted the reeds, the center of the house was named
Nicah. And from that time those reeds were called
Cañas Vivas, or Living Reeds.

Thus the boy-gods exalted the memory of their father and uncle. And they spoke to the spirits of their
father and uncle: "You will be honored by the sons of
dawn, by the civilized peoples; you will be the first to be
praised. Your names will not be lost. So be it! We are
the avengers of your death, of the pains and grief these
caused you."

Then at midday they were raised to the sky, Hunahpú and Ixbalanqué. And one became the sun and
the other the moon. Thus they lighted the arch of
heaven and the face of earth. And they dwelt in the
sky. And so ends the story of Hunahpú and Ixbalanqué.

THE
WAGERS

—Tortoise, come to sweep.
—I have no head, I have no feet.
—Tortoise, come to clean.
—I have no head, I have no feet.
—Tortoise, come to work.
—I have no head, I have no feet.
—Tortoise, come to eat.
—Here is my head, here are my feet.

One day 'Mana Tortoise made a wager with 'Mano Monkey. " 'Mano Monkey, I'll bet you a hand of bananas and a bottle of wine that I can beat you climbing that tall ceiba tree."

'Mano Monkey laughed. "*Caramba*, 'Mana Tortoise, that's not possible. You beat *me?* Well, well. Yes, I'll take that bet. But remember, 'Mana Tortoise, it was your suggestion, not mine."

The two began climbing. 'Mano Monkey wove himself through those branches faster than a coati, faster than a puma. He reached the top of the tree and set himself to swinging on a branch. He swang and he swang and he swang.

Meanwhile, 'Mana Tortoise was puffing her way through leaves and twigs and vines, slowly . . . slowly . . . slowly. By the time she reached 'Mano Monkey, he had swung himself dizzy.

"I see you arrived first," said 'Mana Tortoise pleasantly, fanning herself with a leaf.

"First!" cried 'Mano Monkey with a scornful laugh. "I could have made the trip fifty times and still have won."

"That's possible, that's possible," agreed 'Mana Tortoise, nodding. "You are a speedy climber, 'Mano Monkey. There's no room for doubt. Indeed you have won the wager. I owe you one hand of bananas and one bottle of wine."

'Mana Tortoise and 'Mano Monkey continued rocking back and forth on their branches till 'Mana Tortoise had caught her breath. Then she asked, " 'Mano Monkey, what would you say to another wager?"

'Mano Monkey stopped swinging. "*Bien,* 'Mana Tortoise, what have you in mind?"

"This time I'll wager you *two* hands of bananas and *two* bottles of wine that I can reach the ground faster than you can."

Of course 'Mano Monkey accepted promptly. What a feast he would have with three hands of bananas and three bottles of wine!

"*Uno, dos, tres,* go!" cried 'Mana Tortoise. Pulling her head and feet into her shell, she threw herself into space.

Fast as 'Mano Monkey was—fast as a serpent, fast as a hummingbird—by the time he had swung himself to the ground, there was 'Mana Tortoise waiting for him.

Unlike 'Mano Monkey, 'Mana Tortoise neither poked fun at her adversary nor laughed at him. She did say in an amiable manner, "Well, 'Mano Monkey, two hands of bananas and two bottles of wine—which I won—minus one hand of bananas and one bottle of wine—which you won—leaves only one hand and one bottle for you to pay."

And pay, 'Mano Monkey did. While 'Mana Tortoise munched her bananas and sipped her wine, 'Mano Monkey sat on a branch. He thought and frowned and frowned and thought. He could not convince himself that pokey 'Mana Tortoise could beat him at *anything*.

TÍO RABBIT
AND THE BARREL

One day when Tío Rabbit was on his way to visit
his grandmother, he came face to face with Tío Jaguar.

"I am going to eat you!" roared the jaguar.

"A foolish idea that would be, Tío Jaguar. Look at
me. Skin and bones, no more. If you wish a fine meal,
wait a little. After one month at my grandmother's, you
won't recognize me. 'A rabbit?' you'll ask. 'No, no, a
sheep at least. . . .' Let me go on, Tío Jaguar, and
you'll see."

Tío Jaguar consented, and Tío Rabbit went on his
way, skipping and frisking like dandelion down. But
not for long. Whom should he run into but a lion.

"I am going to eat you, Tío Rabbit," said this king
of the jungle, flashing his powerful teeth.

"Well, well, if you wish, Tío Lion. But it would be
a great mistake. When I return from my grandmother's
in a month, I will make you two juicy meals instead of
one skimpy one."

"Very well then. But make sure you return by this
same road."

Tío Rabbit scampered off with a hop and a jump. A little later he happened on a hungry fox who licked his mustaches on seeing him.

"Tío Rabbit, say your prayers, for I am going to eat you."

"I cannot stop you, Tío Fox, if you are set on such a rash course. It may be better so, for in a month, when I return from my grandmother's, you won't be able to stretch your mouth around me."

Tío Fox grinned greedily. "Oh, I'll wait a month, Tío Rabbit. Just don't forget to return by this very road."

"That's what I'll do," Tío Rabbit promised, and he played follow-the-leader with himself all the way to his grandmother's.

At his grandmother's Tío Rabbit filled himself with fresh lettuce and carrots and cabbage and watermelon. He increased his size by twice . . . no, thrice. His own mother would not have known him.

When it was time to go home, Tío Rabbit jumped into a barrel, which began to roll downhill. It had not rolled far when it encountered Tío Jaguar.

"Tell me, little barrel," said he, "have you seen anything of Tío Rabbit?"

From inside the barrel Tío Rabbit called, changing his voice:

> "The mountain's on fire!
> Tío Rabbit's made tinder.
> Run swiftly, Tío Jaguar,
> You'll burn to a cinder."

Tío Rabbit and the Barrel

Tío Jaguar, believing the mountain to be really burning, turned and fled down the path. Tío Rabbit, in his barrel, rolled after him.

In a little, the lion appeared. "Listen, little barrel. In your travels have you come across Tío Rabbit?"

Again Tío Rabbit, in a shrill, unrabbit-like voice, called from the barrel:

> "The mountain's on fire!
> Tío Rabbit's made tinder.
> Run swiftly, Tío Lion,
> You'll burn to a cinder."

The lion, all alarmed, leaped down the mountain as if the fire were reaching for his tail.

Farther on, Tío Rabbit in his barrel nearly rolled into Tío Fox. "Listen, little barrel, have you seen Tío Rabbit in the neighborhood?"

Tío Rabbit, making his voice deep and gruff, sang out:

> "The mountain's on fire!
> Tío Rabbit's made tinder.
> Run swiftly, Tío Fox,
> You'll burn to a cinder."

"Don't try to fool *me*, Tío Rabbit," said the crafty fox. "First I'm going to pluck you out of the barrel. Then I'm going to eat you up, ears, tail, voice, and all."

His mouth watering, Tío Fox ran after the barrel. But already the barrel was far ahead of him and rolling faster than he could run.

The lazy voice of Tío Rabbit floated back, "*Adios-ito, adiosito*, Tío Fox. Good hunting. Watch for me next year—when I come home from my grandmother's, I may be bigger than you!"

THE
SISIMIQUI

Once, in Guanacaste, there was a town lying at the foot of a mountain—an unhappy town. Each time a young man of that town married, the same night of the wedding he was left without a wife. It so happened that during the night, down from the mountain would slither the Sisimiqui, a horrendous monster, to carry off the girl. He would bear her away to his cave, which was hidden in the deepest folds of the mountain. There she remained, for no one dared to go looking for her.

The young people went about with long faces. No one wished to marry for fear of the Sisimiqui. Why do so when the monster appeared punctually to bear off the bride and she was never seen again?

However, one youth, Juan Valiente, was resolved to marry. And marry he did. But in spite of his being Juan Valiente, bravest of the brave, and sensible, too, that night his bride was removed as easily as a pea from its pod. What a tragedy!

Instead of carrying on, as the other grieved bridegrooms had done, Juan Valiente decided to smuggle

himself into the mountain. There he would search out
the Sisimiqui, overcome him, and release from the cave
all the stolen girls. An ambitious boy, Juan Valiente.

Speaking and acting together, Juan Valiente
seized his *machete*. Armed with it, he and a group of
village youths set out for the mountain of the Sisimiqui. They walked and they walked and they walked.

High in the mountain they came upon an eagle.

"Where are you headed, Juan Valiente?"

"To the cave of the Sisimiqui to rescue the girls
who were stolen."

"I will go with you, but through the air," said the
eagle.

They continued their journey into the mountain.
After some time they encountered a lion.

"Where are you off to, Juan Valiente?"

"I go with my followers to the cave of the Sisimiqui in search of the girls who were stolen."

"I will go with you to do battle with the Sisimiqui."

Juan Valiente's face brightened. It is always a
pleasure to have a lion on *your* side rather than on the
other. They struggled forward, into the deepest wrin-
kles of the mountain. After a while whom should they
meet but a tiger.

"Where will your travels lead you, Juan Valiente?"

"Hopefully to the cave of the Sisimiqui, where I
may find the girls he has stolen."

"I will accompany you and throw myself against
the Sisimiqui."

Juan Valiente smiled. An eagle, a lion, a tiger—all make excellent allies. The group went on its way, climbing up and up and up and . . . up. Across their path hopped a rabbit.

"Is it a pleasure trip you are taking, Juan Valiente?"

"What an idea! We go together to the cave of the Sisimiqui to free the stolen girls."

"With your permission I should be most happy to go with you."

Although everyone knew that one cuff from the Sisimiqui would send a rabbit spinning like a planet, they all admired his spirit.

Juan Valiente answered, "If your pelt has lost its comfort for you, by all means join us."

And they kept climbing, upward and onward, into the heart of the mountain. When at last the cave of the Sisimiqui came into view, they stopped.

The eagle said to them, "Wait here. I will see if the Sisimiqui is awake or asleep. When his eyes are open, it means that he sleeps. When they are closed, he is awake. I will go ahead and advise you."

The eagle swooped away. Soon he returned. "Quickly, run into the cave. The Sisimiqui sits with eyes open, soothing himself with a snore."

Scarcely had he spoken when Juan Valiente, crossing himself, made for the cave and, silent as an ant, crept inside. There he found his bride bathing in a sea of tears. Signaling her to be quiet, he picked her up and carried her outside. He was halfway to his friends when the eagle, who was standing guard at the entrance, sprang up and cried, "Listen, listen! The Sisimiqui wakes! Make ready, make ready!"

In truth, from the noise one would suspect a hurricane to be turned loose on the mountain. There was a crashing of trees, a shiver of fallen rocks and boulders.

The lion cried, "Onward, all of you, while I engage the Sisimiqui!" And he sat down and waited. Swirling like a tornado through the mountain came the Sisimiqui.

"Halt!" roared the lion.

"Who dares to command me?"

"I come to see who is the stronger!"

Scarcely did the Sisimiqui glimpse him when slash, smash, swash, squash! and nothing was left of the poor lion but little pieces.

The eagle, who had remained hidden high on a branch, flew to the escaping townsmen. "He has killed the lion! Make ready, make ready, he is right behind you!" And indeed they heard the storm of a collapsing forest close behind.

"Run, run, I will fight the Sisimiqui!" cried the tiger. The eagle settled on a branch to watch the second struggle. The Sisimiqui appeared, more furious than a bull with a twisted tail.

"Halt at once!" screamed the tiger.

"Who dares to give me orders?"

"I, who come to find out which is the abler."

The Sisimiqui leaped on the tiger and in two times two made rags of him.

The eagle skidded down the wind and called to

the men, "Now he has destroyed the tiger! Make ready, make ready, he is five steps behind you!"

The rabbit said, "Hasten, hasten, leave the Sisimiqui to me." And he lowered himself from his mount, which was an armadillo. The men, seeing him so resolute, left him to his fate, and the eagle stationed himself on a branch to see the quick end of the poor rabbit.

The rabbit turned to the armadillo. "Brother, dig me some nine tunnels in the earth, all of which run together." Then while waiting for the thunder of sound to reach him and for the armadillo to scoop out the nine tunnels, the rabbit took his knife from his sash and inserted himself just inside the first tunnel.

Suddenly there appeared the Sisimiqui, leaping and blowing sparks like a bonfire.

"Halt then!" called the rabbit from his tunnel.

"Even yet someone dares to command me? Who then are you?"

"It is I," called the rabbit, "come to see which of us is the wiser."

"Which is the wiser? Only wait, and you will see!"

And the Sisimiqui pounced on the rabbit. No, not *on* the rabbit but *toward* the rabbit . . . for the rabbit, who was the quickest of the quick, dropped down one tunnel, came up through another, which was behind the Sisimiqui, and cut off the monster's tail. The Sisimiqui made a whirl that shook the mountain and turned his burning eyes on the rabbit. No, no . . . on what *was* the rabbit. The rabbit flew up through another tunnel and cut one of Sisimiqui's paws.

95

The Enchanted Orchard

Breathing fire and ashes, the Sisimiqui stuck his snout into the tunnel where the rabbit was standing . . . or had been standing a moment before . . . but the rascal was already through the maze and out another tunnel to smack the Sisimiqui in the eye.

Well, this sort of business went on and on until the Sisimiqui had nary a centimeter of space on him that was not tinted black, blue, and purple. So weary was he that he could scarcely twitch an ear. Well, what did the rabbit do but pop out of the earth and with his *machete* slice off the Sisimiqui's head.

With one flutter the eagle reached Juan Valiente and screeched, "Stop, companions, stop! The rabbit has killed the Sisimiqui!"

They hardly dared believe it, but the eagle related how the thing had happened.

Juan Valiente reached the rabbit first, and when he saw what the smallest of all of them had done, he embraced him while the others congratulated him.

At once they returned to the Sisimiqui's cave, and each one carried out his bride. And still there were girls left over. Of course they decided to have a *fiesta* and celebrate the end of the Sisimiqui.

There is no need to add that the guest of honor at the frolic was the rabbit. Everyone made much of him, and one girl whispered that she might be coaxed into marrying him. But that was not for the bachelor rabbit. He was more frightened of one girl than of a troop of Sisimiquis!

THE
CEGUA

One night a city dweller was walking from town to a ranch in an isolated area of Costa Rica. There accompanied him a *campesino*, a countryman, forthright and simple. Not a shred of wind brushed the trees. No one passed them on the road. Nothing broke the silence except the clump of their boots and a little stream that stumbled noisily over the stones in the depths of a nearby valley.

All at once they heard the approach of a trotting horse, its hoofs muffled by the grass.

"Someone is coming," the city man said to his companion.

But the old fellow, with the keen hearing of the countryman, answered, "He travels not by this road but by the one higher up."

Almost at once the hoofbeats ceased as if the horseman had reined in his mount. A minute later he must have resumed his journey. Only in place of trotting, the horse was now running at full gallop.

The Enchanted Orchard

In a solemn voice tinged with respect, the *campesino* muttered, "Ah, the unfortunate one has come on the Cegua." Then he continued, "Have no fear, master, she will not confront *us*. We are two, and besides that, we are on foot."

"The Cegua?" the city dweller exclaimed. "What sort of animal is that?"

The other smiled slightly as if unwilling to believe such ignorance. "But, *Señor*, is it possible that you, who read so much, do not know what the Cegua is? It is a form of the devil, and heaven keep you ever from meeting with her."

"I know nothing at all of the Cegua. Do me the favor of explaining."

They were already near the ranch, so they could hear the stamping of the horses, the barking of the dogs. The night was fresh; the moon and stars showered the vast countryside with their pale silver light. It was the time to hear of mystery and dark happenings.

The old fellow began, "No one who has once seen the Cegua is ever again the same. Men strong, tanned, and healthy, who think nothing of working twelve hard hours a day, become thin and loose-skinned and yellow after viewing the Cegua. Some have died of pure fright." He went on to name those in his memory who had lost their lives because of this terrible being.

"One is not able to see her everywhere," he went on. "There are certain places she prefers. Along here she walks often. For that reason, you can imagine, it is rare to find a horseman riding alone. Always two ride together."

"Cannot two people see her?" the other interrupted.

"She appears to one alone," he answered.

"A place far from towns and dwellings, especially if there are trees and the road is narrow—that is where she likes to surprise travelers. In the middle of the road she presents herself, and in a sweet, weak voice, as if she were dying, she says, '*Señor,* I am so tired and I must go to see my mother who is ill. Would you be so kind as to take me to . . .' and she names the nearest town, because of course she knows everything."

"Then she has the appearance of a person?" the city man asked.

"True. She is a beautiful girl, fair-complexioned, with dark eyes and curling black hair and a red, red mouth. All who see her are charmed by her and saddened by the weariness of her face and voice."

A breeze came to stir the still air and flutter the leaves. Someone might have been standing there, breathing through the foliage . . .

"No one can resist her plea. Some carry her on the saddle before them, others behind. It is all equal to her. When they begin to ride, she turns her head if she is in front. If behind, she makes the rider twist to look at her. And what does he see?

"The beautiful woman is no more. For a face she has the skull of a horse. Her eyes flash fire. She bares monstrous teeth. From her mouth comes a vapor smelling of rotting things. At the same time she clings like a wild animal to the rider. The horse himself, as if know-

ing what he carries on his back, bolts in such madness
that no one can stop him."

"And then what happens?"

"Those whose minds are filled with evil die without exception. They are found lying broken on the

ground, their eyes open. The rest, as I told you, are so changed that from then on they serve for nothing."

And that is the tale of the Cegua. The children of Central America believe it. The grownups, no, of course not, what nonsense . . . but all the same, they are careful, when they ride in lonely places, always to go two and two, just in case.

THE
DROWNED MINE
OF SANTA ANA

A story says that in the region of Santa Ana, in Costa Rica, there exists an enchanted mine. Strange tales are told of what can be seen there. I listen to the tales. To view the mine itself, I have no desire. Spirits and spells are better described than experienced. . . . Then white hair does not appear overnight, years do not depart in terror from one's life.

But back to the mine. A hundred years ago it was unenchanted—sadly so. This most ordinary of mines belonged to a foreigner, a fellow with a fondness for money. Fondness has a gentle sound. Let us change that to *locura,* or madness, for money. Madmen are capable of a degree of shrewdness.

This owner was shrewd in his business dealings. One day he called together the considerable number of Indian slaves he used to work the mine.

"On my word of honor," he announced to them, "the very day you bring me gold from the mine, I promise you your freedom. On the same day. Now, to work, to work. Gold is what we are searching for. Remember that. You bring *me* gold, I give *you* freedom."

The Indians, exhilarated by the promise, returned to work. And work they did. Not a game of gambling stones, not a *siesta,* interrupted their efforts. They were as desirous of their liberty as the master was for his gold. (I told you he was a shrewd one.)

To the satisfaction of everyone, gold appeared. Not a mere nugget or two, either, but gold in quantity. The Indians, overjoyed, hastened to inform their master.

"Master! *El oro*—it is here. Much of it. The mine is rich with gold. And now—we are free?"

On seeing the gold, the owner was struck with a double attack of his ailment. "Free? Free?" he asked. "But if you go free, it means this fine gold will remain attached to the mine. And so attached, it will help me not at all. No, no, my good people, on the contrary, you must work harder than ever. The gold must be taken out, melted down, and then poured into bars to store in my storeroom." He heard the Indians murmur and went on.

"As for freedom—think no more of it. A thankless state. One must then worry himself over food, shelter, a bit of clothing. As it is, I worry about these things for you. The trouble I take to find the whitest rice, the largest and plumpest *frijoles.* . . . Think you that other masters take such pains? No, my children, be grateful for such rich living as I provide. And now, to work, to work!"

The Enchanted Orchard

The Indians wasted no breath on protests. Instead, they conceived a plan, which they put into effect that same night. They deflected the course of a river, now known as the River of Gold, into the main shaft of the mine. The tools, the machinery, the equipment were all buried under the flood and destroyed.

Content with their vengeance, the Indians fled. Scattered like birds through the jungle, they were as impossible to capture.

The master? Perhaps he was seized with true madness. At all events, he, like the Indians, disappears from the story.

To this day it is said that on a clear night three tremendous balls of gold have been seen to roll about the deserted fields near the mine. From their movements it appears that a giant amuses himself playing marbles with them.

If one approaches the mine, he hears peculiar noises and frightful explosions inside. (The teller-of-tales covered his ears and screwed up his face to show me how dreadful they were.)

I have even been told that in the largest tunnel one can glimpse a magnificent crystal palace. Inside, seated on a throne set with rubies and diamonds, a beautiful princess wearing jewels and a dress of sky blue spins with a golden distaff.

And what have princesses and strange sounds and giants to do with Indians and a gold mine? Who knows? I merely said the mine is enchanted . . . and there is no explanation for enchantments.

AN
ANCIENT CURSE

"Over spilled blood, stone will leave stone."

So goes an old saying in Spanish. In other words, on the spot where a man has murdered someone, no building will stand. Either it will not arise . . . or if it is already there, you can count on its falling down fairly soon.

In Cartago, one of the larger cities of Costa Rica, the saying is known by each and every inhabitant. They recite it to all visitors, shaking their heads mournfully but with pride. The truest saying there ever was, they assure you.

"Look," they say, pointing to the church . . . rather, to what would be the church if. . . . Anyway, they point to some quite impressive ruins. "There is the proof."

By now you are quivering with curiosity to hear the sinister story—it *must* be sinister, dealing with blood and fallen stones. . . . And so it is, affirms any Cartagoan. Eagerly he tells you how it happened.

The Enchanted Orchard

Back in 1575 two brothers with the name of Madrigal arrived in Costa Rica. Both were unmarried. One came as priest of the parish and the other came . . . well, who knows why he came, to seek his fortune, to see the world, or maybe for no reason at all.

After a time the bachelor brother, the one who was not the priest, fell in love—not at all surprisingly, as Costa Rican girls have the reputation of being remarkably beautiful. What *was* surprising was that the priest also fell in love. What was utterly astounding was that it was with the same girl. Problems, problems, problems.

The girl solved the problem nicely by falling in love with the secular brother. Well and good. Things were really falling his way. Number one, he had a sweetheart. Number two, being intelligent and likable, he had just been elected mayor of Cartago.

Now let's look at the priest. *Nothing* seemed to be going right for him. No girl. As he was a priest, he couldn't have married her anyway, but he doesn't seem to have thought of that. Then his brother, for whom he had developed a rabid jealousy, was nominated for a high office. Instead of rejoicing, the priest fell into a decline. He did his best to prevent the election. His attempt failed. When the brother was elected, the priest was in, oh, such a state—a bad enough state to make him lose his reason.

On the first day of January, 1577, the young Madrigal was to be sworn into office. Solemn ceremonies. Speeches. A high mass. Candles and prayers.

At the door of the church the mayor-elect and his committee were met by the priest and his assistants, who were to lead off the day's events by giving a blessing. As Señor Madrigal lowered his head, the priest pulled out a dagger. Venemously he drove it into the heart of his brother. The mayor dropped dead at his feet.

The uproar was all an uproar should be. Not only had murder been committed—it had taken place in a *church* by a *priest*. While the onlookers stood paralyzed by horror, the priest escaped through a side door. Outside, his servant was waiting with a strong horse. Off went the priest, riding like the wind across the hills to freedom.

The rough ride must have bounced some of that lost reason back into his head. At León de Nicaragua he presented himself to the authorities and confessed his crime. He was returned to Cartago and tried. Repentently enough he paid the penalty.

However, it seemed that payment was not enough. It might have been for an ordinary run-of-the-mill murder. But a sacrilegious murder? *That* kind refuses to be paid for.

A few years later, due perhaps to age, the church fell apart. Fortunately it happened at night, and no one was hurt. The church was rebuilt. An earthquake shook it to the ground. The church was again reconstructed. Again it fell down. After another attempt or so, the priests had learned their lesson. They put a church somewhere else.

But some people just won't give up. In 1841 a fine cathedral was built on the site of the ill-fortuned church. On September 2, the day of its benediction, an earthquake came along and . . . you can guess what happened to the cathedral.

Some years later an ambitious architect planned a church capable of resisting time, fire, and divine wrath, no matter where it was located. It went up in that choice site which was meant from the beginning for a church (so said the enthusiastic architect). The walls rose, the stones remained docilely in place, the Cartagoans went about saying at last the blood was washed away, the curse was lifted. . . . The earthquake of 1910 unhinged the stones, broke the ligaments of mortar, and left them jumbled on the ground.

It was an eternal lesson, say the Cartagoans, looking affectionately at the broken stones spouting flowers and vines and grass, that the blood of the brother would never be erased, that the place would remain cursed for century upon century. A long time, perhaps. But you know how ancient sayings are—they last a long time, too.

HOW
THE DEVIL
CONSTRUCTED A
CHURCH

The town of Curarén is one of the most ancient in Honduras. It was who knows how many years old when the Spanish arrived from across the sea. And that was—let me think—over four centuries ago. Today Curarén still stands, the home of a famous church. The story of this church bears telling.

Some years after the Conquest, the Curarenes (which is another way of saying the inhabitants of Curarén) were ordered by the Spanish governor to build a church in their village. The townsmen were quite content at the thought of a fine church. At the thought of constructing it—piling stone upon stone upon stone upon—they quite contentedly fell asleep.

Time after time they put off the construction. At last, in a fit of rage, the governor decreed that if the church were not completed within a week, inside and out, upside and down, the town would be destroyed— totally destroyed.

It was a distressful business. "An impossible task,"

groaned the mayor. The members of the town council beat their heads against the ground. Without doubt it was farewell to Curarén—Curarén the ancient, the beautiful, Curarén their home. A pity!

There loomed one hope. Their Indian neighbors to the north informed the town that the *Enemigo Malo,* the Devil, had himself fashioned the Bridge of Slaves in Guatemala. Surely the Curarenes could reach an agreement with him to build their church?

The townsmen shuddered. But—a decree is a decree. The church—or destruction.

It was done. The Devil wrote the contract, and the mayor signed it with the blood of his veins. Both parties were committed. On the one hand, the Devil was to construct the church, even to applying a coat of plaster both inside and out. On the other hand, as his tribute, he would be presented annually with a certain number of unbaptized babies.

During the night of construction the Curarenes were under strict orders to stay inside their homes; only the mayor and town council would remain on watch to make sure the work was well done. The walls would be of stone masonry and the stone would be unadorned. No carving. No embellishment. Even at a price, the Devil had his limits. Of course, the church must be completed before the most diligent cock could crow his morning song, "Christ is born"; otherwise, the work was forfeit.

One councillor rubbed his hands together. "No one can build a church in one night," he whispered. "Even the *Enemigo Malo.* We are quite safe."

But the mayor was troubled. "He's a shrewd one. You don't often hear of *him* losing a bet. And if he wins . . ." The mayor shivered. "I'm afraid he'll manage. And then what?"

The councillors were silent. The "then what?" was too horrible to consider.

On the agreed-on night the work began at dusk. Enormous stones were heard to roll down from the hills. The demon workers hammered and cracked and chipped and smashed, making an infernal racket. Children cried. Dogs howled. Women wept. The uproar within nearly equaled the uproar without. The hours passed, as stone was sandwiched on stone, with lime smeared in between.

The Devil stood by, grimly counting the minutes. The walls rose—but not too quickly. Impatiently the Evil Enemy ordered that to save time larger stones be used at the top to complete the walls. On went the roof and belfry. Up swung the bell. Splash went the plaster as it was mixed.

The race was as good as lost. The number of industrious demons guaranteed that. Already the interior of the church was plastered. Only the outside walls remained.

Where was morning? Was it lost among the shadowy hills of night? The councillors trembled from skull to tarsus, thinking of the terrible promise they had made. Better that the Spanish had razed the village.

But just when the workers began slapping the plaster on the outside stones, there sounded that loveliest and most welcome of songs, the "*Quiquiriqui,*

111

Christ is born!" A moment later it was followed by a thunderous clap as the enraged Devil fled to the Inferno with his legions.

The Curarenes sighed with tremendous relief. Then they looked about. "Why is it so dark?" whispered one.

Perplexed, the mayor answered, "I don't understand it. Not one silver thread of dawn do I see. The east is as black as the west, and both are as black as— well, as night."

"So they are, so they are," croaked a voice from nearby. "I always wanted the chance to outsmart that old rascal."

Holding a candle, Tía Luisa hobbled into view. Between cackles of laughter she told of her trick.

In her hut, which stood close to the church, she had remained awake throughout the night. In one hand she held a candle and in the other a cock. When, well before dawn, the swishing sound of paintbrushes reached her ears, Tía Luisa had lit the candle. Then, naturally, the rooster had crowed.

The gruff old governor, visiting Curarén, approved the church. (He was not informed of either the bargain or the builders.) His only objections were that the largest stones were set at the top of the wall rather than at the bottom, and the church was well painted inside but not out.

The mayor explained that they had tried to plaster the walls, but the plaster refused to adhere and peeled away. As for the large stones, the governor could

understand—the laborers had been in a hurry, a fiend-
ish hurry (the mayor winked slowly), so that some of
the stones were set helter-skelter, here instead of there.

But so what, the church had resulted altogether well, no?

"Oh, altogether," replied the governor. Surely the laborers had toiled night and day? The work had gone particularly quickly at night, the mayor admitted.

And that is the story of the church of Curarén. Except that not long ago a bolt of lightning struck the church, singeing the image of Saint Luke.

"Ah," exclaimed an old lady, chuckling, "Satan has never pardoned us for winning *that* bet."

THE
PURCHASED MIRACLE

There once lived, in the district of Lempira in Honduras, a gentleman dedicated to business whose name was Don Juan. Business in Lempira was not bad, not bad at all. To say the least, Don Juan was well-to-do. To say the most, he lived in a fine house, rode a spirited horse, ate tender chicken stewed with rice, day in and day out. He lacked nothing—that is, nothing to add to his comfort.

One day Don Juan journeyed to Santa Rosa de Copán, where he had business dealings. He found the town preparing for its yearly pilgrimage to the Church of Esquipulas in Guatemala. The Señor de Esquipulas was famed throughout Honduras and Guatemala for his miracles.

"This thing of miracles . . . what madness!" guffawed Don Juan. "These country people—so needy that a handful of *frijoles* is a feast for them—waste their time chasing after miracles! Better to search for treasure glimpsed in a dream. Even better to *work* for the

treasure. Yes, work. I am, perhaps, a poor example."
He simpered, while his friends assured him that, on the
contrary, he was the perfect example. (It was what Don
Juan thought himself.)

"I may be a poor example, but after years of labor,
often twenty hours a day, I have accumulated a modest, a very modest, fortune. And did I acquire this fortune through running after miracles? What a joke!
Through *work*. Along with some small sharpness of
wit, some native intelligence, a shrewd understanding
of business. . . . But miracles and prayers? A waste of
time."

Don Juan lectured the townsmen in this same vein
and then shook his head with pity—and some annoy-
ance. He had wasted his breath. Not one soul scurried
to sharpen his *machete*. Not one returned to his maize
patch. All was as before—eager preparations for the
pilgrimage to Esquipulas.

However, Don Juan's words may not have gone
unheeded. Who knows? Having completed his dealings, Don Juan returned to Lempira. There he was
stricken with convulsions, then dizziness. Afterwards,
pains here, there, and elsewhere, in his right ear, his
left toe, both elbows, his shoulder. At last these strange
symptoms culminated in a fever, which left Don Juan
blind—totally blind. Such a pity! Blindness lends no
advantage to a businessman.

His family and friends cared for him tenderly.
They prayed for his quick recovery. Don Juan made no
sharp remarks about the waste of prayer, the gain of

work. No, indeed. But then he could hear the prayers and could no longer see the work.

With little to do, he found more time to listen to the supplications of his family. A prayer to the Señor de Esquipulas? Don Juan was desperate. Foolish these prayers might be, but then again. . . . He promised that if the Señor would return his sight, he, Don Juan, would join in the next pilgrimage to Esquipulas. Moreover, to demonstrate his faith, he would leave there his heavy gold watch valued at three hundred *lempiras,* its chain of gold for which he paid thirty *lempiras,* a watch charm of a gold eagle costing a hundred, and an ancient medal of pure gold worth a hundred and fifty *lempiras.* Don Juan was not a man of half measures.

The following year, when the annual excursion was planned, Don Juan was the first to register. He was a changed man. "Woe is me!" he said with a sigh. "How misery does uncover one's mistakes. I, who believed one's work to be the supreme virtue, am converted to absolute faith. Gold? A useless luxury. Miracles? They are beyond price."

Don Juan made the pilgrimage from Santa Rosa to Esquipulas, accompanied by his wife and children. The walk was long and painful. Don Juan stumbled often. His family entertained him with tales of miracles the Señor had performed for the believing. Don Juan grew daily more cheerful. To prove his faith, he was trudging for miles over an uneven road scattered with sharp stones. He was offering a respectable gift. His family's

entreaties were mixed with his own. Surely a pair of
new eyes was not too much to ask for? Not of the
Señor de Esquipulas, who granted favors of all
sizes . . .

The Purchased Miracle

At the church Don Juan left his watch and chain, his charm, his gold medal. He made his devotions with unaccustomed humility. Suddenly he experienced a great dizziness. His head felt like a cage with a wild dove trapped inside. Instead of a miracle, he was dying. . . . His wife helped him to the inn. Here Don Juan tumbled into bed with a raging fever. He was soon sound asleep.

The next day he felt much better. Well enough, in fact, to return to the church. He repeated his prayers. All at once he felt his eyes water with such force that he drew out his handkerchief to dry them. Shadows passed back and forth before him.

"The miracle! Is it happening? Is this, then, the miracle?" gasped Don Juan. And he closed his eyes and sat with them squeezed tight shut for some time.

When he opened them again, he could see as well as in the days of his youth. A miracle it was, his family exclaimed. They lost no time in spreading the splendid news throughout Esquipulas.

Days later the pilgrimage returned to Santa Rosa. Don Juan had quickly adjusted himself to his good fortune—ay, no, what am I saying—to his tremendous miracle. His mind dwelt lovingly on miracles. A sudden thought of his business . . . no, no, it was miracles he must think of. Business . . . miracles . . . business . . . mira . . . business.

Someone in Santa Rosa asked, "My dear Don Juan, what were your feelings precisely in experiencing this overwhelming miracle?"

Don Juan blinked. "Miracle?" he asked vaguely.
"But, man, I felt nothing, nothing at all. There was
nothing to feel. It was simply that the effect of that
fever finally wore off. My sight returned—quite naturally. By chance it happened during our visit to Esquipulas. By pure chance." He chuckled. Then his face
grew long.

"I had planned to consult a doctor in Mexico. An
expensive operation. When eyes are concerned, you
know. . . . However, I ended by making a more painful and costly trip." He shook his head dismally.

"And how is that, Don Juan? A trip more costly
than one to Mexico? Explain yourself, please."

"This so-called miracle has cost me more than a
trip abroad. Look you, I gave in payment a gold
medal, a charm, a fine watch attached to a gold chain,
all valued at more than five hundred *lempiras*. Miracle
indeed! At least it is paid for, in full."

Don Juan and his family left Santa Rosa for Lempira. For this journey they used their horses' legs, not
their own. Don Juan recovered from his gloom slowly.
The cost of such a pilgrimage. It was fantastic. Still,
with cunning trade and bargaining he would soon buy
himself another watch, a chain, a charm for the watch,
a medal . . . much finer than those he had left with the
Señor . . .

Don Juan felt a burning in his eyes. He rubbed
them. There was the sensation of sand inside them. His
vision dimmed. In terror Don Juan tried to find his
handkerchief. In his pocket his trembling hand encoun-

tered the famous gold watch and chain, the charm, the ancient medal . . .

When they reached Lempira, they found all the townsmen gathered, desirous to learn of the miracle. But Don Juan, blind as a coconut, shut himself in his house. There was time to spare for meditating on miracles.

NOTES
ON THE STORIES

The Enchanted Orchard and *The Warrior Who Shot Arrows at a Star* (Honduras) are taken from *Leyendas y Tradiciones Indígenas* by Pedro Aplícano Mendieta, Librería Atenea, Tegucigalpa, Honduras, 1967, and included in this collection with the permission of Pedro Aplícano Mendieta. I translated and adapted both to appeal more to young people. *The Warrior Who Shot Arrows at a Star* is interesting not only for the situation but also for the Mayan and Aztec customs it describes.

The Boy with the Hand of Fire (Costa Rica) is taken from *Las Semillas de Nuestro Rey*, narrated for children by Carlos Luís Sáenz E., Las Américas, San José, Costa Rica, 1958, which contains legends of the aborigines of Costa Rica. *The Boy with the Hand of Fire*, a tale of the Guatuso Indians told by Amando Céspedes M., is so simply and vividly told that I translated it quite literally. It is included in this collection with the permission of Carlos Luís Sáenz E.

Nandayure and His Magic Rod (Costa Rica), told by Anastacio Alfaro, is an amusing legend of the Chorotegas, which I rewrote. It is also taken from *Las Semillas de*

The Enchanted Orchard

Nuestro Rey by Carlos Luís Sáenz E. and is included here with the permission of Carlos Luís Sáenz E.

The Treasure of Nosara (Costa Rica), also a Chorotegan legend, was told by Miguel A. Vidaurre and is adapted. It, too, is found in *Las Semillas de Nuestro Rey* by Carlos Luís Sáenz E. and included in this collection with the permission of Carlos Luís Sáenz E.

The Lagoon of Masaya (Nicaragua) is a legend of the region of Masaya in Nicaragua that I translated and adapted from *Panorama Masayense* by Enrique Peña Hernández, Talleres Tipográficos San José, Managua, Nicaragua, 1957 and is included in this book with the permission of Enrique Peña Hernández.

How the Moon Came to Be (Guatemala), a comical myth of the beginning of the moon, the Milky Way, and whooping cough, comes from "Li Poo" (The Moon), adapted from *Guatemala Myths* by George Byron Gordon, by permission of the University Museum, Philadelphia, Pennsylvania.

The Beginning of Maize and *The First Flute* (Guatemala) are two stories that I found tucked away in a travel book, *Land of Eternal Spring: Guatemala, My Beautiful Country,* by Lily Aguirre, and that I have freely adapted.

The Creation of Man, The Tricks of Hunahpú and Ixbalanqué, The Message, The Revenge, and *The Mission Ended* (Guatemala) come from the *Popol Vuh,* the ancient sacred book of the Quiché Maya Indians of Guatemala. I translated the stories from the Spanish version of Adrian Recinos, Fondo de Cultura Económico, México, D.F. México, 1964, and these five stories are included in this collection with the permission of Maria P. de Recinos. Sr.

Notes on the Stories

Recinos' translation is so beautifully done that my adaptation consists mainly in telescoping certain chapters. *The Tricks of Hunahpú and Ixbalanqué* and *The Message* are literal translations of the myths.

The Wagers (Panama), a funny little tale of 'Mana Tortoise and 'Mano Monkey, is taken from *El Folklore Panameño en Función de las Teorías Freudianas* by Luisa Aguilera de Santos, Imprenta Los Andes, Santiago, Chile, 1963, and is included in this collection with the permission of Luisa Aguilera de Santos. This version closely follows the Spanish.

Tío Rabbit and the Barrel (Panama) is one of the many Tío Rabbit, or Uncle Rabbit, stories common throughout Latin America. Tío Rabbit is known for his mischievousness, his ingenuity, his cleverness, his ability to keep the jungle in an uproar. The tale is also adapted from *El Folklore Panameño en Función de las Teorías Freudianas* by Luisa Aguilera de Santos and is included in this collection with the permission of Luisa Aguilera de Santos.

The Sisimiqui (Costa Rica) is another tale of adventure centering around the rabbit, found by María Isabel Ruiz de Sáenz in Guanacaste, a region of Costa Rica. It is taken from *Las Semillas de Nuestro Rey* by Carlos Luís Sáenz E., Las Américas, San José, Costa Rica, 1958, and included in this book with the permission of Carlos Luís Sáenz E.

The Cegua (Costa Rica), a "ghost story" of the Cegua, or Tzegua, was written by Máximo Soto Hall and included in the book *Leyendas de Costa Rica*, compiled by Victor Lizano H., Soley & Valverde, San José, Costa Rica, 1941. I adapted the story.

The Enchanted Orchard

The Drowned Mine of Santa Ana (Costa Rica) was adapted from a story written by José Bustamente and included in *Leyendas de Costa Rica*, compiled by Victor Lizano H.

An Ancient Curse (Costa Rica) is a story I heard told many times in Costa Rica while I lived there. This version, which I adapted, was written by Jaime Granados Chacón for a Costa Rican newspaper and later included in *Leyendas de Costa Rica*, compiled by Victor Lizano H.

How the Devil Constructed a Church (Honduras) I adapted from the book *Patrios Lares* by Pompilio Ortega, Imprenta Calderón, Tegucigalpa, Honduras, 1951, and is included in this collection with the permission of Leonor Ortega Vda. de Molina and Carmen Molina de Hepburn.

The Purchased Miracle (Honduras) I found and adapted from *Cosas de la Vida Real,* by Florencio Alvarado, Imprenta de la Policía, Tegucigalpa, Honduras, 1951, and it is included in this collection with the permission of Florencio Alvarado F.